RAGE AGAINST
THE MACHINE
STAGE FIGHTERS

PAUL STENNING

Published in 2008 by
INDEPENDENT MUSIC PRESS
Independent Music Press is an imprint of I.M. P. Publishing Limited
This Work is Copyright © I. M. P. Publishing Ltd 2008

Rage Against The Machine – Stage Fighters
by Paul Stenning

British Library Cataloguing-in-Publication Data.
A catalogue for this book is available from The British Library.
ISBN: 978-1-906191-07-8

Cover design by Fresh Lemon.

Dedicated to Isla

Printed in the UK.

Independent Music Press
P.O. Box 69,
Church Stretton, Shropshire
SY6 6WZ
Visit us on the web at: www.impbooks.com
and www.myspace.com/independentmusicpress
For a free catalogue, e-mail us at: info@impbooks.com
Fax: 01694 720049

Rage Against The Machine

Stage Fighters

by Paul Stenning

Independent Music Press

CONTENTS

ACKNOWLEDGEMENTS

Special thanks to Garth Richardson, Ben Myers, Rey Oropeza, Mumia Abu-Jamal, Chris Poppe and Martin Roach.

Prologue

The wiry figure crouches as low as he can, stunted dreadlocks glistening in the stage light as he gradually rises and starts to unleash vocal fury upon the thousands in attendance. Behind him the band plays a riotous mix of post-hardcore-meets-rap ferocity as Rage Against The Machine begin to hit a groove few bands could ever match. They play their set, speak their message and get the fuck out of the building. Another stage trodden, another missive spoken. Another successful show, and many new fans have been gained.

That's what it's all about for this band and over the years their cause – of political justice and freedom of speech amongst many other noble strivings – has alerted countless young men and women to the problems in the world, whether it be the unjustified incarceration of Black Panther Mumia Abu-Jamal or subjects closer to home, such as domestic poverty and sweatshop labour conditions.

If you are a big Rage Against The Machine fan, you know where you were when you first heard them. Their impact is simply immeasurable. From the moment they erupted onto the rock scene in 1992, they have broken boundaries left and right whether it be with their innovative musical artistry or their frequently incendiary lyrics and riotous performances. They have spoken out more than other artist in hard rock history against the many capitalist injustices we all face and have truly assaulted the mainstream, realising their potential power several times over.

Though they took a long sabbatical in which three of the four members started a new band – Audioslave – Rage Against The Machine never lost their impetus, making an impact with all posthumous live releases and continuing to drag people into the political activism arena as more and more new fans discovered their four stunning studio albums. Then in 2007, the band reconvened with its original line-up to once more scare the worldwide establishment. No one knows what will happen next but it's fair to say the band have clearly had enough time off and believe now is truly the moment to effect the most obvious and positive change.

This book focuses on the art, message and history of Rage Against The Machine. It also follows the post-Rage work of all members, be it Audioslave or the more low profile years for singer Zack De La Rocha in which he frantically worked on his long-mooted solo album. It is a work which encompasses all that Rage Against The Machine stood, and continue to, stand for. With this in mind, it naturally focuses on the political background to the band and their upbringing both before, during and after their RATM catalogue. As the band have often stated, it is difficult, if not impossible to separate art from politics. With such an obvious, politically-minded band it would be lazy and indeed misguided to skirt around the political background to their career and the precipitating events of not only the 1960s and 1970s where the members grew up, but the historical context which enveloped their youth – primarily the fact that they were of different ethnic backgrounds.

Whether you are interested in politics or not, if you are a Rage Against The Machine fan you cannot avoid the issues the band campaign for. Though guitarist Tom Morello has acknowledged the power of the music of its own accord, stating, "A Rage Against The Machine show is not a college lecture," the band's statement in accordance with their musical proficiency cannot be avoided. Indeed, without this multi-dimensional message geared towards society, RATM would be a completely different band – and perhaps not quite as loveable.

I have tried to cover all bases with this book, both musically and politically. We also have to remember not everyone is a political scientist and some basic explanations are necessary for a lot of the history told. For anyone already heavily involved in emancipating their minds and learning as much about the truth of the world as they can that's great, but for those who are just beginning on their quest there is a list of recommended reading and viewing at the back of the book.

The mere fact you are holding this book in your hand is an

achievement for freedom of speech. Perhaps it will go by unnoticed in the chasms of the establishment, but within these pages are the seeds of a righteous cause intended to make you think, research and look towards changing the world around you. It starts with a spark and it can start with you. Our remaining civil liberties are in danger of being eroded, or possibly already have been, in many instances. The wrong word here and there can make you outlawed by mainstream society. So this one is for other outcasts, free thinkers and freedom fighters, potential or realised.

I trust you will read the book with an open mind and a true sense of our capabilities to change ourselves and the world around us. Rage would have wanted it that way.

And if you don't see yourself as the next Malcolm X or you're simply not interested in the political views of the Rage Against The Machine members, don't worry – this is also a book about a great rock band.

Paul Stenning, June, 2008.

Chapter One
Protest And Survive

To assess the nature of a political band, we must first understand what politics really means. The dictionary definition explains the word to principally mean, *"The art or science of government or governing, especially the governing of a political entity, such as a nation, and the administration and control of its internal and external affairs."* When looking into the meaning of this, we see that essentially every single aspect of our daily lives comes down to politics. The price of a CD is politics, just as much as a war for oil.

Everything comes down to politics, so when a band is defined as political it is really nothing more than a case of commenting on the society around them. Unless an artist only sings about their own emotions, as soon as their reflections concern society in any small fashion, their actions are politically defined.

Some see politics as boring – and at a government level, for most of us it would be. This is why only certain types of people can stomach such a job, or have the required focus to be involved. They are often dull, thus it convinces us that politics in itself is dull and we should not be concerned with it, leaving other people to make key decisions and manipulations over which we have no control or interest. We give them that power virtually before they even start.

So a band who tag themselves as political are instantly saying to us, 'We must look at certain issues, or even all issues, politics concerns *us*.' You wouldn't let other aspects of controlling your life go, so why should we let our fundamental rights and living conditions be controlled by an entity out of our reach and out of our control? Yet by definition of the establishment, political bands are often seen as dangerous, just as peace protestors are, or anyone who does not conform to mainstream society. Anything or anyone who challenges the established norm is seen as a threat by the system because at any stage these mavericks and revolutionaries can alert people – the blind mass of society – to the injustice going on around them, and make them understand that they are not really free in the way they presume.

Freedom of speech is a basic right, one to which we are less entitled than we may think. Yet somehow, when those freedoms are tested by a band, standing on a stage engaging the audience with loud, messianic music, that freedom seems more dangerous than ever to the establishment. If you can say anything, then anything is possible and this scares the powers-that-be to death. Politics is no more boring than sports, it is the people involved in politics who make it boring, because that is their design.

As controversial author David Icke says, "Politics, now there's a funny thing. It comes from the word 'poly', meaning many and 'tics' meaning blood-sucking insects. Ironic isn't it?"

All fundamental issues and human rights are important to each one of us and in examining the society in which we live, we will instantly find inequality, unfairness, disparity and discrimination. Bands who speak out on such topics are merely doing the job the politicians are supposed to do, alerting the general population to the ills of society and demanding we all do something about it. People are becoming inexorably more aware that we cannot allow the powers-that-be to dictate our lives any longer and that we, personally, have the power to change our lives. Bands who exert this message of freedom – such as Rage Against The Machine – are a danger to the establishment and therefore must be silenced. Yet it is our right to hear everyone's point of view and to take politics into our hands. Politically motivated bands are a good start. It is in fact a sad reflection of society that there are very few overtly political bands in existence, and even fewer who have actually changed the status quo or truly challenged the system.

Music reflects the society it pervades and it only goes to prove that many of us are not as politically minded as we should perhaps be. The rumbles of protest music which have resonated over the decades serve as constant reminders and inspiration to push the boundaries and question authority. Though many presume they know what's best for us, the reality is almost always the complete opposite.

In order to understand the lineage of a protest band such as RATM, it is important to focus on where they came from. Not just their experiences growing up or their immediate influences as musicians but where they truly *came* from – the merging of the 'motherland' with the 'land of the free'. Without the struggles and tremendous art which emerged from the centuries preceding the birth of Rage Against The Machine, the group may not even have existed, certainly not in their present form. Therefore we must first briefly trace the history of political and protest music.

No history book would teach the life and times of opressed people better than a listen to the last hundred years of recorded music. For example, black artists and musicians spoke the truth in a form that at the time was still known as entertainment. As long as it was dressed up in a tune that was acceptable, they could communicate an awful lot of subversive messages. The success of whole genres of music and entire labels (like Motown or Stax) devoted to a certain style, gave license to particular artists and their message. It didn't take a full career devoted to a political statement to upset the status quo and artists or bands with only one or two songs of powerful sentiment are just as important as those who based their career on it.

The history of black protest music began with the songs sung by African-American slaves in America during the 19th Century. They often sang with just a banjo for company, an instrument which was created by enslaved African-Americans, and was later appropriated by the white man and used for folk music. Yet its origin was in spiritual music, usually gospel and often the songs were created as a subdued lyrical protest to those who had enslaved them.

At the end of the 1800s, African-American music had permeated the mainstream American psyche and performers of the time, such as Scott Joplin were popular ragtime artists. Joplin and his ilk became associated with the work of early civil rights activists and were also the soundtrack to the Harlem renaissance, one of the most significant eras in African-American history.

In 1925, writer Alain Locke composed a book which would

spawn the movement and give new credence to the views and rights of the African-American. He became unofficially known as the father of the Harlem Renaissance. *The New Negro: An Interpretation* was a focus on the African-American way of life and the achievements of the people, within art, music and literature. It was a celebration of black culture and a positive outlook for an uprising and a blueprint for a healthy future.

From this book came many more which celebrated the African-American culture, mostly based in the Harlem area of New York City. Yet its impact went beyond this, covering the entire United States. According to Professor Paul P. Reuben, a world expert and academic who has written widely on the subject, "The Harlem Renaissance was more than just a literary movement: it included racial consciousness, "the back to Africa" movement led by Marcus Garvey, racial integration, the explosion of music particularly jazz, spirituals and blues, painting, dramatic revues, and others."

Blues and jazz were two forms of music dominated by black musicians and it was through these mediums that music as a whole began to change. There are few musicians in the world today who do not have a huge amount of respect for the likes of Miles Davis and John Coltrane. Though possessed with a deep, haunting voice, Billie Holliday also permeated the white mainstream with her unique take on jazz and blues. She also used her fame to assert the tragic lament of 'Strange Fruit', a poem about lynching whose melody and lyrics were written by the Jewish school teacher Abel Meeropol.

"Black bodies swinging in the southern breeze, strange fruit hanging from the poplar trees," Holliday mourns. "Pastoral scene of the gallant south, the bulging eyes and the twisted mouth."

The dictionary definition of lynching reads, "To execute without due process of law, especially to hang, as by a mob." Lynching was rife in the latter part of the 19th Century but it would continue well into the 1940s and even beyond. Black men were most frequently lynched for 'crimes' against whites. A study by Ida B. Wells (an early civil rights activist) contested that in many cases there was little basis for these so-called crimes, which were often exaggerated or did not even happen at all. The most common accusation levelled against black men was the raping of white women. (Wells incidentally was a courageous, fearless campaigner for equal rights and 40 years before the infamous Rosa Parks refused to give up her seat on a bus to a white person, Wells had done the very same thing – more later).

The principal exponent of lynching was the Ku Klux Klan (or KKK) and a study of vigilante justice covering 1868 to 1871 noted the Klan were responsible for more than four hundred lynchings. Their violent ignorance gave license for some white racists to also seek out their own form of 'justice'. It would take almost until the end of Billie Holliday's life for the lynching culture to end and even when she made the issue known to a wider audience there was a subliminal apathy in response. As Holliday said, "They'll ask me to 'sing that sexy song about the people swinging'."

Eventually, through the tireless campaigning by many prominent black commentators, from protests and marches to magazine articles and books, lynching would finally be seen for what it was, inhumane, bigoted violence.

Thanks to musicians such as Holliday, Davis and Coltrane, black culture was slowly starting to infiltrate the white establishment. The likes of Louis Armstrong were also held in high regard by the mainstream and Armstrong would remain famous and revered long after his death in 1971. Yet in many ways and to some observers, Armstrong was subservient to the mainstream, seemingly a man who knew his place and perhaps believed that place was still as a partial slave, making money to please and appease the white man, always with a stunning smile on his face.

One man who had a similar charisma and likeability to Armstrong but was very much an outspoken protestor was the singer and civil rights activist Paul Robeson. He was a highly educated, multi-lingual man. His bass singing voice (the deepest range possible) was immensely powerful yet beautiful and the songs he made with that voice sounded all the more poignant with Robeson behind them.

In 'Born To Be Free' he declares, "You can wreck my name, vilify me, stretch me on the rack, but I won't bow down to any man, be he white or be he black … I stand here struggling for the rights of my people to be full citizens in this country and they are not! Rise up, my brothers and sisters, we were born to be free."

With Robeson's notoriety, he had the means to make a political impact and in 1946 he made a brave stand against lynching by aggressively campaigning directly to then-President Harry S. Truman. Robeson claimed that if the government did not step in to resolve the senseless killings then black people would fight back.

Truman had set his stall out a year before in a speech to congress when he claimed "Every segment of our population, and every individual, has a right to expect from his government a fair deal." It was now time to back up that assertion.

In 1946 Robeson founded the American Crusade Against Lynching, an organisation dedicated to educating the masses and stopping the violent vigilante groups. This was the move that the white establishment had long feared; though they were probably surprised it had taken so long. When the likes of white physicist Albert Einstein lent his name to the cause, the self-law for white vigilantes was all but over. Without Paul Robeson however it may have gone on for far longer. He inspired many people of his generation, white and black, and was the mentor for another civil rights activist who took the Robeson template and put it to further good use.

Singer Harry Belafonte was a black vocalist who managed to permeate the masses with his calypso songs, yet behind the scenes he was a fellow activist, campaigning for civil rights and other humanitarian causes. He belonged to the Civil Rights Movement of the 1950s and became one of Martin Luther King's close associates. In more recent times, Belafonte has been prominent in his criticism of the George W. Bush administration.

The burgeoning black music scene of the late Fifties through the Sixties was also responsible for an upturn in societal viewpoints, bringing black faces to living rooms all over the United States and beyond. With the formation of the Stax and Motown record labels, there was an influx of tremendous music and a new understanding of black culture. Suddenly many whites, who had perhaps previously feared those of a different colour, saw them as no different to themselves. The first steps towards integration and acceptance were being made.

Motown Records would become an immense success, featuring some of the best known and most loved soul artists of all-time, and its impact continues to this day. Formed by Berry Gordy, it was the first label to feature African-American artists, be run by an African-American and spread over to commercial areas and become successful throughout white society. The list of legendary artists is lengthy and includes The Temptations, Gladys Knight & The Pips, The Jackson 5 and The Supremes.

So the barriers were being broken down, yet discrimination continued. The Motown style was known as soul or rhythm & blues. As one eminent music critic once suggested, if The Beatles had been black they would surely have been known as an R&B band but because they were four good looking white boys, they were a 'pop' band.

Stax meanwhile released records by artists such as Isaac Hayes and Albert King but would also release material by comedian Richard Pryor and the Reverend Jesse Jackson. At the Wattstax music festival of 1972, known as the African-American Woodstock, Jackson took the stage and read his poem, 'I Am Somebody', affirming: "I am – Somebody. I may be poor, but I am – Somebody! I may be on welfare, but I am – Somebody! I may be uneducated, but I am – Somebody! I must be, I'm God's child. I must be respected and protected. I am black and I am beautiful! I am – Somebody! Soul Power!" Seven years after the race-fuelled Watts riots, the concert brought together thousands of black people, with tickets selling for only a dollar.

While Motown in particular assaulted the mainstream, other less immediate artists continued the civil rights crusade, while simultaneously creating classic music. Curtis Mayfield led his charge of gospel-derived soul, lending weight to the civil rights crusades. Many of his songs were positive reaffirmations of black pride, with titles such as 'Move On Up' and 'People Get Ready' with its "There's hope for all" tag-line. Marvin Gaye and Stevie Wonder were of the same era as Mayfield but both enjoyed more popularity, and both also made many references to the civil rights cause.

Mayfield's influence ran deeper into the movement than his peers – partially because of this, his popularity has always remained secondary to the likes of Gaye and Wonder. Still, his impact was felt through the black power movement and his 'We're A Winner' mantra became one of the movement's chief weapons. In that song Mayfield sings: "We're living proof in alls alert/That we're two from the good black earth/And we're a winner."

This track, along with his 'Keep On Pushing' anthem were strong accompaniments to the times. When James Brown released 'Say It Loud – I'm Black And I'm Proud' in 1968, the song's popularity was immediate and the impact enormous. Here was a well known soul singer who had overseen hits such as 'Papa's Got A Brand New Bag' and 'I Got You (I Feel Good)' which white music fans all across the world knew well, and he subverted the mainstream with a direct call to arms for black pride. As Public Enemy front man Chuck D has said, "We went from coloured to black overnight."

Many other artists included anti-racist sentiments in their repertoire. One of the chief protagonists of rebellious soul/funk was Sylvester Stewart, better known as Sly Stone, leader of Sly & The Family Stone. He oversaw tracks such as the call to power of 'Stand!' and the uncompromising 'Don't Call Me Nigger, Whitey'. Unfortunately the potential rebellion of the band was somewhat diluted when Sly was harassed by certain black militants who insisted he sack the two white members of the band and attempted to influence his material towards a more aggressive black militant stance.

Perhaps one of the best known political musicians is Bob Marley. Though his politics were often concerned with his country of birth, Jamaica, his lyrics transcend cultural nations and boundaries and can be applied to the black empowerment as a whole, particularly the likes of 'Get Up Stand Up' ("Stand up for your rights") and 'Redemption Song' ("Emancipate yourselves from mental slavery, none but ourselves can free our mind, redemption songs – all I ever had, these songs of freedom.")

In America, as the pioneering DJ technique of the likes of Grandmaster Flash and DJ Kool Herc gave way to the beginnings of the rap genre, expanded by the vocal beat box rhythms made by Doug E. Fresh and Biz Markie, a whole new generation of music was born. Rap was occasionally aggressive but always thought provoking and in the early Eighties sounded fresh and exciting. There were no limits and no one who could remotely rhyme or talk fast enough was excluded. Yet, it was almost exclusively a black movement. When white rappers jumped in on the act it was frequently disastrous (see the likes of Vanilla Ice) and prevented other white rappers from attempting to fit in. This balance was only (moderately – after all it was only initially one man) redressed by the emergence of Eminem at the turn of the 21st Century.

At its inception, hip-hop was largely a young person's domain and as such inspired the black youth of America, and beyond. As the soul/jazz singer Joy Denalane says (in the *Get Up, Stand Up* documentary) of her growing up in Germany, "I was pushed down the stairs at school and called nigger, nigger pig, duck arse, all sorts of things, the one with the ugly hair. Nobody wanted to know me or anything about me and even the boys had no interest at all in me. Al that changed when hip-hop happened. Hip-hop was something I clung onto because somehow it represented people like me and suddenly it was cool to be like me."

Which brings us, finally, to Rage Against The Machine. The rebellion of hip-hop was a powerful inspiration for many disaffected youths growing up, not least a young poet named Zack De La Rocha. "I was listening to hip-hop early on growing up," he told *Rolling Stone*, "and I had a lot of white friends who refused to talk to me the second I put on an Adidas sweat suit and was breaking, or I was walking through campus with my radio playing Eric B. & Rakim and LL Cool J and De La Soul. To so many whites it was just noise. To me, it was people reclaiming their dignity."

White protest music is generally seen as a separate entity to that of black protest art, though the two have crossed over occasionally, and many sympathise with the others' point of view. Still, the lineage of Rage Against The Machine would not be complete without tracing the background to the white artists who have also spoken out against injustice through musical history. Where white and black protest music meet, you will find Rage Against The Machine.

But before them we have to go back – way back – to the first truly successful white protest group, an American family singing four-part harmony group known as The Hutchinson Family Singers, who were active in the 19th Century. They were extremely inflammatory for their time, covering such topics as women's rights, equal rights, social reform, activism, the Temperance movement and abolitionism – all in a gentle, soothing manner. The group even sang at the White House in the 1840s for democratic president John Tyler and were later championed and became friends with progressive future president, Abraham Lincoln.

In the late 1800s, Joel Emmanuel Hägglund, better known as Joe Hill, caused mayhem for the American authorities and was subsequently put to trial for murder. He was an Industrial Workers Of The World (IWW – essentially a labour union) activist and travelled the nation singing songs of protest. RATM guitarist Tom Morello would later reference Hill in 'The Union Song' for his The Nightwatchman project.

In the early 1900s, a man named Woodrow Wilson Guthrie was born and would later make a career as a folk singer and musician under the name Woody Guthrie. His most famous song, 'This Land Is Your Land' was a direct protest at what he saw as the blind jingoism of the unofficial American national anthem, 'God Bless America' which Guthrie viewed as too simplistic and unrealistic. Guthrie's song referenced the false sense of empowerment given in 'God Bless America' by sneering sarcastically at the end of his musical retort: "I'd seen my people, as they stood there hungry, I stood there asking, is this land made for you and me?" Again, Tom Morello would later pay homage to this particular songwriter, and his most famous song, when he performed it as part of The Nightwatchman live set.

Guthrie was also pro-union and was infamous for bearing a constant slogan on his guitar which read 'This Machine Kills Fascists'. He was wide ranging in his protest topics, speaking out against the racist treatment of 28 Mexican immigrant farm workers who had been returned to their country after a plane crash on American soil. Guthrie felt the way the Mexicans were not referred to by name, merely as "deportees" was unethical and racist. He wrote the bittersweet irony of 'Deportee' to make a fitting statement.

Another of Guthrie's best known tracks is 'The Ballad Of Tom Joad', the protagonist being a fictional character created by writer

John Steinbeck in his classic novel *The Grapes Of Wrath*, which focused on the Dust Bowl migration. Joad embodies the common man who must deal with injustice by becoming politically active and inspiring others to work together. Guthrie wrote his song after viewing the movie inspired by Steinbeck's novel, and said, "[It] shows the damn bankers' men that broke us and the dust that choked us, and comes right out in plain old English and says what to do about it. It says you got to get together and have some meetings, and stick together, and raise old billy hell till you get your job, and get your farm back, and your house and your chickens and your groceries and your clothes, and your money back."

Another set of folk musicians, The Weavers, became famous as protest singers, specifically banjo player Pete Seeger. The notoriously left-wing band were in support of workers unions which their songs referenced. They would not play many of their more controversial songs live, yet still they were under surveillance from the FBI. Because of this they were blacklisted on many popular radio and TV networks during the Fifties as part of McCarthyism – the era of anti-communism and Soviet suspicion of Americans during the Forties and Fifties. Joseph McCarthy, after whom the term was named, was famous for installing the Hollywood blacklist where he conducted hearings and investigations into so-called subversive artists, actors and musicians. Many of these were purposefully denied work due to their perceived or actual radical beliefs. For the likes of The Weavers, this meant a severe decline in popularity and eventually they were ostracized by their record label, Decca.

Pete Seeger, who was once a US Communist party member, continued his protests unabated and became one of the most revered folk musicians of the 20th Century. It was he who largely popularised the famous civil rights chant of 'We Shall Overcome'. True to his own beliefs, he didn't think The Weavers should undertake any activity which fell into the corporate dictatorship and when the band decided to perform a jingle for a cigarette commercial, he left the group.

Inspired by Woody Guthrie, Seeger adorned his banjo with the motto, 'This Machine Surrounds Hate and Forces It to Surrender'.

Seeger was an early advocate of Bob Dylan who was to become one of the most famous protest musicians of the last 50 years. Out of a frantic period of politically-inspired compositions came several classic songs which still resonate with meaning today.

Some of his best known protest songs include 'The Times They Are A Changin'', 'Masters Of War', 'Blowin' In The Wind' and 'Talking World War III Blues' and he also made reference to a racist killing (white murdering black) in 'The Lonesome Death Of Hattie Carroll'. Dylan was often likely to play down his role as some kind of generation spokesman. For instance where his song 'The Times They Are A-Changin'' was viewed as a satirical take on the burgeoning age gap and culture differences of disparate groups in the Sixties, he shrugged off such assumptions saying, "I didn't mean 'The Times They Are A-Changin' as a statement ... It's a feeling."

Though Dylan was heartfelt in his lyrics and sentiment, and certainly in his activities − such as joining in at rallies of the Civil Rights Movement − it seemed he was indeed viewed more as a generation spokesman and protest singer than even he actually believed. Soon he would alter his image, tidying up and buying expensive clothes, and shunning the notion of protest folkie. Yet he is still seen today as one of the most prominent and important voices of the Sixties and beyond.

Thee Vietnam War provided prime fodder for the views of musicians and artists, much like the Iraq war of the 21st century has inspired great swathes of protest literature and music. There were many singers and artists who spoke out against the invasion of Vietnam. In some cases, it was perhaps a little contrived on the part of certain artists, usually those who only seemed to make one song about the subject. But nevertheless the breadth of opinion went far and wide into the musical community. Everybody from The Doors and Black Sabbath to Jefferson Airplane and Buffalo Springfield made their telling statements in certain songs.

Two of the most prominent protest artists associated with both anti-Vietnam rhetoric and other protest actions were Joan Baez and Phil Ochs. Baez, half-Mexican and half-British, became known as a protestor on a large scale when she performed 'We Shall Overcome' during Martin Luther King's 'March On

Washington'. She was then perpetually linked to protest and civil rights marches and showed great courage when she openly spoke out against withholding taxes to pay for war. The figure commonly associated with use for military action from the average tax costs was 60% and Baez withheld this amount of her income tax in 1963. She also encouraged resistance of the draft (avoiding the otherwise accepted reality of being sent to war without a choice) and was even jailed for a month in 1967 for blocking the entrance of the Armed Forces Induction Center in Oakland, California. Later that year after her release, she spoke to 30,000 people at a free concert called the March 1966 Fifth Avenue Peace Parade at the Washington Monument. Together with protest singer Phil Ochs, Baez celebrated the end of the Vietnam War in May 1975, with a huge celebration under an umbrella which stated Ochs' persistent motto of 'The War Is Over'.

Ochs is one of the best known white protestors of his generation and was in the public eye, getting on the establishment's nerves up until his early tragic death at the age of only 36 in April 1976. Essentially a folk singer, Ochs had been influenced by the likes of Woody Guthrie and Pete Seeger but managed to create plenty of memorable work himself. Chief among his best known compositions were the likes of 'Draft Dodger Rag', 'Love Me I'm a Liberal', 'Ringing of Revolution', and 'I Ain't Marching Anymore' whose lyrics perfectly represented the anti-war era.

Ochs was a familiar figure at protest rallies and civil rights marches and organised many labour events during his short career. Though he was undoubtedly a protest singer, he viewed himself as a 'topical singer' but was outspoken with regards to the nature and aim of a protest song, stating bluntly that "a protest song is a song that's so specific that you cannot mistake it for bullshit."

The peace rallies of the Sixties gave way to the asinine glam rock scene, which though fun, was a million miles away from the protest scene. The advent of punk rock brought a new definition of protest though it was less political and more of a statement against the establishment as a whole. Only certain artists spoke out against particular injustices or causes, chief among them were The Clash. A precursor to ethically-sounding bands like Fugazi, The Clash charged reasonable prices for concert tickets and albums.

Whereas much punk derived its anger and reaction from the basics of anarchism, the likes of The Clash managed to speak out with a more considered, and more international approach. Importantly, they would become a huge influence on Tom Morello.

The Clash were the first white band to both support the oration of the black nation whilst simultaneously endorsing the need for white youth to rise to such activism. With lyrics indicative of the time, they were an inspiration to disaffected youth and provided a noble alternative to the skinhead culture which permeated many youth areas of England at the time.

The Clash were brimming with statements of disaffected life in the inner city as well as outward protests to the world and society at large. So many of their songs made comment on social injustice, whether 'White Riot', 'Atom Tan', 'Washington Bullets', 'Guns Of Brixton' or 'London's Burning'.

The Clash were also staunch supporters of the Anti-Nazi League and in one of their most famous shows they headlined the Rock Against Racism concert of 1978 where they played to 80,000 people in London's Victoria Park. In 1980 they would release their *Sandinista!* album, which was titled in deference to the Sandinista National Liberation Front, whom they supported, along with other Marxist movements. The SNLF was a Nicaraguan organisation, originally formed by students in 1961 and they were to revolt against the US-supported right-wing dictatorship established by Anastasio Somoza. They overthrew Somoza and ruled Nicaragua for 11 years. The Clash were anxious to remain 'a band of the people' even as their career grew and fans multiplied. They would seek to keep a friendly, respectful relationship with their followers, welcoming fans backstage after gigs.

A more extreme proposition to emerge in The Clash's era were anti-establishment punk pranksters Dead Kennedys, an American quartet who formed in 1979. Their stance was fiercely anarchistic, yet wrapped in the supremely intelligent, humorous and sardonic lyrics of Jello Biafra. He was born Eric Boucher but developed the name of Jello, as a nod to an American institution/brand name of Jell-O and combined it with Biafra, a Nigerian state whose inhabitants suffered mass starvation − the irony of a manufactured mass food production and the horror of famine. Biafra's lyrics were always clever and often sarcastic, taking the role of the perpetrators he wished to expose in songs such as 'Police Truck' and 'Kill The Poor'.

The band were staunchly against the accepted machinations of the music business, or at least Jello Biafra was (he would later fall out with his former band mates over royalty arguments and his insistence the band should not bow down to corporate sloganeering or cash driven reunions).

For the Bay Area Music Awards of 1980, the Dead Kennedys were invited to perform due to the organisers seeking some 'new wave credibility', despite the fact DK were a punk band. The band were originally scheduled to play their 'hit' 'California Über Alles' but opted to cause a furore, when, 15 seconds into the song Jello Biafra shouted, "Hold it! We've gotta prove that we're adults now. We're not a punk rock band, we're a new wave band."

In a move which would later see a parallel with a stand taken onstage by Rage Against The Machine when they protested against the right-wing Parents Music Resource Center, the Dead Kennedys appeared all dressed in white shirts with black dollar signs adorning their fronts. They scrapped the performance of 'California...' and instead played 'Pull My Strings', an attack on the immoral mainstream music industry. Later, in a move which pulled the strings of the PMRC, the Dead Kennedys released their *Frankenchrist* album with so-called obscene artwork included inside the record cover.

The front cover itself was a swipe at the Illuminati (a fabled global order of 13 chief families whose power and wealth means they effectively control world affairs; it is even said that the US President reports to them) as it featured the strange creatures who inhabit the meets for the obscenely rich and powerful. Yet inside the record was the real problem – a painting by H.R. Giger, which featured several penises involved in sexual intercourse. The band were charged criminally with distribution of harmful matter to minors and Jello Biafra's apartment was raided and searched by government agents.

Bands such as the Dead Kennedys – and frontman Biafra in particular – were not so much advocate of protest songs as possessed with an ability to make innate protests with their very presence. Everything that spilled from the mouth of Biafra was challenging and subversive to the mainstream. But perhaps the real cause of such distress amongst the music moguls and companies were lyrics which portrayed the music machine for the vacuous sham it really was. Some of Biafra's best lyrics came on the *Frankenchrist* album, in the form of 'MTV Get Off The Air'.

"My job is to help destroy what's left of your imagination," Biafra whips mockingly, "By feeding you endless doses of sugar-coated mindless garbage."

For their incendiary music, fast paced, high-pitched yet catchy songs, and their challenging, educational lyrics, the Dead Kennedys have to be the ultimate protest punk band.

As we have seen, the notion of political protest through music is nothing new but despite all the inspiring and progressive art which has emerged over the years, there was going to be one band that took that protest to new levels and established it within such a framework that every race, colour and creed could feel part of it and rally against any area within the corruptive system that they so desired. A band who would change the face of music and build foundations for mass change which they are still pushing today. They were influenced by the multitude of black and white musicians who came before them but, for the Nineties generation and beyond, this would be the most politically outspoken and rebellious act to speak of. To borrow a phrase from Ice T – they seek truth, justice and fuck the American Way … Rage Against The Machine.

Chapter Two
Too Black, Too Strong

The mid-Sixties were a tumultuous time for race relations in America. Though Martin Luther King and Malcolm X were very public figures, there seemed to be no end to the racial hatred plaguing the black nation. In May 1964, two black men, Henry Hezekiah Dee and Charles Eddie Moore, were hitchhiking in Meadville, Mississippi when they were captured by members of the Ku Klux Klan. They were kidnapped and beaten to death. It took two months for anyone to find them, by which time their bodies were severely decomposed.

The KKK is a white supremacist group, founded on the belief that American white Protestant males are superior to people of colour. Their most notorious area of operandi, especially during the first century of their existence (they formed in 1865), was the oppression of – and violence toward – ethnic minorities. During their existence they have been found responsible for killing many in the name of what is effectively ethnic cleansing, a warped ideal by which they believe they can turn America into a white-only country.

Elsewhere, in June 1964, Nelson Mandela, a black activist in South Africa, was arrested and sentenced to a lengthy prison term. He would end up serving 27 years for varying charges of 'terrorism' relating to his work with the African National Congress (ANC). He later became President of South Africa and is revered as one of the most courageous and inspirational human beings of the 20th century.

On July 18, 1964, there were race riots in Harlem, New York City. Demonstrators gathered to protest the seemingly unpunished fatal shooting of a 15-year-old African-American male, James

Powell. He was killed by a white police officer. The Congress of Racial Equality (CORE) approved of the protest, which was initially peaceful. Yet after violence occurred between certain protesters and the police present, the protest became a riot, in which mass violence, looting and general chaos occurred. For another two nights the mayhem continued, even spewing into the Brooklyn neighbourhood of Bedford-Stuyvesant. Sadly, one person was killed and more than a hundred injured as a result of the riots. More disturbingly they precipitated a further series of race riots later in the decade, most notably the clashes in 1965 in Watts, Los Angeles, which led to the deaths of 34 African-Americans.

In between these aberrations in black history, came the birth of a man who was to become one of the most prominent black artists of the Nineties and beyond. Thomas Baptist Morello came into the world in a Harlem hospital on May 30, 1964. His parents were an unusual coupling. His Caucasian mother Mary was of Irish and Italian heritage whilst his father Stephen Ngethe Njoroge was the first ambassador from Kenya to the United Nations. Stephen's uncle, Jomo Kenyatta, was the first elected President in Kenya and served for 18 months. Kenyatta was an immensely intelligent politician and, like many of his generation, he was more concerned with the freedom and basic rights/necessities of African peoples than ruling or division. He was a reliable source of quotable material and was the author of several books. One of his more famous quotes reads, "When the missionaries arrived, the Africans had the land and the missionaries had the Bible. They taught how to pray with our eyes closed. When we opened them, they had the land and we had the Bible." Kenyatta lived until he was 86 and passed away in his beloved Kenya.

Morello's father was part of the Mau Mau uprising, in which Kenya attempted to gain independence from the British Empire (they succeeded in December 1964), yet those who were part of the insurgency referred to themselves as Muigwithania ("The Understanding") or Muingi ("The Movement"). Nobody knows for sure the meaning of the term Mau Mau but it was possibly a negative connotation spawned by the British. Ngethe Njoroge was certainly a revolutionary which was no surprise given his family's political history and standpoint.

It was equally no surprise that Mary Morello was to meet and eventually marry the Kenyan freedom fighter. She had always advocated equal rights and was a well travelled lady by the time she approached her forties, settling in Kenya for three years where she was to meet her future husband. Mary was born in Marseilles, Illinois in 1924 so it was strange that a globe trotting African history graduate and a Kenyan revolutionary should decide to relocate to Harlem, New York. Their base in the then-crime and poverty stricken borough wasn't to last long. Sadly, Tom only made it to his one year landmark before his mother and father divorced. Mary decided to go to her home state with her young son and settled on a town which was not used to seeing people with anything other than a pale skin colour.

Libertyville is a suburb in the north of Chicago, five miles from Lake Michigan. Mary Morello had been forced to move there because her work as a teacher often presented difficulties. Previously, she could either find work but not be allowed to live in the community due to her black son, or she could live peacefully in an area where there was no work available. The unusual acceptance of this one very small town was therefore gratefully received by the hard-working Mary. She would go on to teach US history and social studies at Libertyville High School.

Even this was relative acceptance, as Tom Morello would later attest, "The real estate agent had to go door to door in the apartment complex where we rented to see if it was OK with people. One reason we succeeded, I think, was because I'm Kenyan. They could use that. Kids would come up to me in fourth grade and say, 'I've been meaning to ask you this, and I don't know how to say it, but are you the prince of Africa?' Seriously. This rumour followed me through my college years. I was nineteen years old, I was on a date, and this kid says, 'I don't know how to say this but are you really the prince of Africa?' I think that germ was started by the original real estate agent who was trying to sell the family to the locals."

Tom Morello would later lay claim to being the first person with "brown skin" to live in the town; he was certainly one of the first, but even in 1960 there were only a grand total of seven non-white residents, making the town 99.9% white.

The 2000 census of Libertyville showed a cosmopolitan improvement whereby the town is now only 92% white. It is certainly not unusual for a white American neighbourhood to be on land taken from American Indians but it's interesting to note that up until August 1829, the Libertyville land was owned by the Illinois River Potawatomi Indians. They were eventually forced to sell their land for which they received $12,000 in cash and $12,000 worth of goods, plus a yearly delivery of 50 salt barrels. By the mid-1830s, the US government had disseminated the native peoples. (Perhaps the most notable historical fact for many however is the fact that Marlon Brando used to live in Libertyville.)

"The politics happen on the playground the first day," Morello said of being in an all white school. "People start name calling and what not. And your mom explains what that is, and she either gives you the Malcolm X speech or the Martin Luther King speech, depending on the day and the size of the opponent."

Tom Morello would later tell *Alternative Press*, "When you're black in America, you are political, like it or not. You have no choice in the matter. When I was six years old, I used to stay at a day-care house when my mom was teaching school. The daughter of the woman who ran the house used to always call me names, 'N-wording' me up and down. I didn't really know what it meant, but I knew that it was bad and that it had something to do with the fact that I was different from her." Morello was upset and eventually told his mother of the bullying one night through fits of tears. He received his first lesson in black history and, newly alert to the work of Malcolm X and other black revolutionaries, knew exactly what to use as a future retort.

"The girl started calling me names again on the next day," he continued, "but this time, I fired off with 'Shut up, Whitey!' and I clocked her with my little fist! It created enough of a commotion so that the day-care woman came over and scrubbed her daughter's mouth out. It's not like I felt particularly righteous or anything. I just kinda thought, 'Hey, that worked!'"

Mary Morello was no stranger to racial controversy. She had been part of the Civil Rights Movement in the Sixties, when racial tensions were at their peak. The movement was popularised by the likes of Malcolm X (real name Malcolm Little) and Martin Luther King. Earlier, in 1955, Rosa Parks also gained notoriety and a permanent place as a civil rights activist after she had refused to give up her seat on a bus for a white person, as was the norm.

The moral of that particular tale concerns the passive acceptance of so called normality. Many black people assumed it was the law to relinquish their seat for a white person on a public bus. They were wrong. It was simply something so indoctrinated in society that it was accepted without question under a false pretence. Only when somebody stood up and refused to acquiesce to the norm did the system come under scrutiny. Suddenly it was realised that all along there was not a single law in place to keep this ludicrous pattern in effect and the whole thing fell to its knees.

Yet a pattern still exists within the embedded psyche of the white population. In the *Malcolm X* movie, Albert Hall's character Baines gives the young Malcolm a lesson in political power. He directs him towards the dictionary and proceeds to point out the glaring differences in the definitions of the words 'white' and 'black'.

Though this was a fictional scene, the parallels with reality are striking and show how deeply rooted the meanings of what is right and wrong sadly often blend too far into colour definitions. Though by their very nature and relevance each colour must have varied descriptions and connotations, it is interesting to note the disparity between the following. Black: *"Characterised by absence of light; enveloped in darkness. Gloomy; pessimistic; dismal. Sullen or hostile; threatening. Without any moral quality or goodness; evil; wicked."*

Whereas the definition of white is: *"Being of the achromatic colour of maximum lightness; having little or no hue owing to reflection of almost all incident light; 'as white as fresh snow'; Morally pure; innocent. Without malice; harmless."*

Mary Morello was also involved with The National Association for the Advancement of Colored People (NAACP) and closer to home the Chicago Urban League. This was a collective of interracial members who assisted African-Americans arriving in Chicago from the deep South. Essentially it is dedicated to helping with financial organisation, employment, education and entrepreneurship. Occasionally Mary Morello would find Ku Klux Klan paraphernalia in her office at school in Libertyville and, one time, there was a noose hung in her garage.

Perhaps unsurprisingly, the Black Panthers were very much discussed in the Morello household and as young Tom grew up, experiencing his own problems with racism and seeing his mother's personal struggles, he gravitated towards the teachings and writings of Huey P. Newton and Bobby Seale, founders of that radical Sixties party.

The origins of the party were based in self defence and self-preservation. As many African-Americans were under threat from the government or white racists within the US, Newton felt the need to establish a party which could unite and rise up in self-protection. The black panther was chosen merely as a symbol of strength and had previously been used by the Lowndes County (Alabama) Freedom Organization, a voting rights group.

Initially the party advocated non-violent self-defence, merely hoping to organise and educate black men into a committee of knowledge and solidarity. The new party outlined a ten point program which established the basic needs and wants of the black people of America. Additionally it underlined that oppression of blacks had to end immediately and that the members would do anything to achieve these ends. Perhaps predictably, such revolutionary talk met instant resistance from the American government who, fearful of a mass black uprising, were quick to outlaw the group. The Panthers were also a threat to law enforcement. At the time of their inception, the numbers of black police officers throughout the country were minimal; they were often outnumbered by a ratio of 10:1. There were eventually conflicts between Black Panther members and the police, and over the course of the next few years 34 Panthers had died from police raids and shootouts. The FBI were to step in and sought to shut down the Panthers and all other organised 'minority' groups. At one point FBI founder and chief J. Edgar Hoover claimed the BP were "the greatest threat to the internal security of the United States."

In one of the better known tragedies involving the party, members Fred Hampton and Mark Clark were shot dead in their sleep due to a raid by 14 Chicago police officers. Others were harmed during the break-in. Clark was killed with a shot to the heart as he sat asleep in a chair. In the United States Court of Appeals, January 4, 1978, a federal grand jury determined that the police fired between 82 and 99 shots while most of the occupants lay sleeping. Only one shot was proven to have come from a Panther gun and this was from Clark's gun, which recoiled as he was shot.

There were many such incidents relating to the Black Panthers and law enforcement and eventually the party would disintegrate due to spiralling legal costs and internal disputes over the direction of the party. Some members are still in prison today due to incidents allegedly connected to their involvement with the party, the most high profile of which is Mumia Abu Jamal who was sentenced to death for the murder of a police officer in 1981. More on Jamal later...

Though the party would become known more for their violent clashes than their politics and desire for positive change (a result of the American historical propaganda machine), their views were clearly understood by many black youngsters growing up in the Sixties and Seventies. As Tom Morello would later explain, "One thing that appealed to me about the Panthers was that it wasn't just an African Nationalist organization. It was about the underlying problems of economic injustice and the 'divide and rule' kind of thing. How, if you keep poor blacks, whites, Chicanos, Koreans, or whoever, at one another's throats, they're not going to realise whose boot it is on the collective neck. It was Newton and Seale who kind of opened my eyes to that."

Clearly the impact of his mother fuelled the Morello fire, and Mary was to remain a constant influence and source of information as her son grew. As future band mate Brian Grillo (singer in the band Extra, and Lock Up with Morello) would later attest. "She's the coolest mother that anybody could imagine having. When we were on the road, she would send him copies of *The Nation* in the mail instead of clean underwear."

As a teenager, Tom Morello would be more influenced by Clash albums than the news, understanding from an early age that the vast majority of media was suppressed, manipulated and nothing but a huge government propaganda machine. There were few – if any – alternative media outlets in Libertyville and so it was through his mother and the musings of an English political punk band that Morello developed a keen sense of social justice and understanding. "I thought the *Sandinista!* record had more accurate and vivid portrayals of US policy in Central America than Tom Brokaw was giving on the news," he would reveal. "And it fired my imagination as well."

Meanwhile many miles away, in Long Beach, California, several years after the arrival of Tom Morello, Zacarías Manuel De La Rocha was born on January 12, 1970. Like Morello, when young Zack was just a year old, his parents split. His time was then divided between his mother in Irvine, Orange County and his father in the Lincoln Heights area of Los Angeles. Roberto 'Beto' De Le Rocha was a Chicano, a Mexican American. There are also conflicting claims however that Beto was an Hassidic Jew, from a Spanish Jewish family. He was certainly a member of Los Four, a group of artists who were responsible in exposing Chicano art to the American people of Los Angeles and beyond.

"They were artists who realised that art as a medium is also very political by nature," his son Zack told *Raygun*. "He would do a series of paintings for the United Farm Workers depicting, like, Mexican history to make it visible to the public. He and the other members, Carlos Almaraz, Frank Romero and Gilbert Lujan, all tried to document that and make it accessible to the community."

In one of many interviews Almaraz, (who has sadly passed away) claimed Beto said, "His family was originally from Spain. And you kind of believed it, that he was a very unusual kind of person, very delicate and very bright, very sensitive, and a wonderful artist." Almaraz would also add, "He had travelled around the world. He actually took a long trip with his wife and family around the world, and had a pretty sophisticated outlook on life, and very, very much of an introvert, individualist."

Zack's father was clearly a sensitive and thoughtful individual; perhaps so wrapped up in creative talents he suffered some form of mental torment, like many artists before him. When Zack was eleven, Beto suffered a breakdown. He destroyed much of his own artwork and went on a forty day fast which left him with permanent mental and physical scars. Ultimately Beto De La Rocha would make a reasonable recovery yet it caused much unexplainable behaviour in the early years of his son's upbringing. According to *Alternative Press*, Zack even developed a slight drug problem as a direct result of his father's mental illness.

The young De La Rocha expanded on the situation with his father. "I'd spend three weekends out of the month at my father's house, eat on Friday night and not eat again until Monday morning when I'd get back to my mother. I was so young at the time that I didn't really question it too much. I love my father, dearly, and didn't understand [what] was happening. I'm not sure that he did, either." The two would often be limited to Beto's apartment with the door locked and the curtains drawn. With no food and no entertainment, Zack was in a very awkward and unenviable position for one so young. It seems, according to some reports, that he had enough gumption to insist he stop visiting his father eventually. He was therefore permanently with his mother in the affluent Irvine, an overwhelmingly white district, in which over 60% of residents are Caucasian, with most of the remaining population Asian-American. As of the 2000 census, there are still only 1.45% black residents residing in the town.

"Living in Irvine, I was pretty much the exception to the rule," Zack would later recall in *Raygun*. "The rule for Chicanos was you were there because you had a mop or a broom in your hand or a hammer, or filled baskets of strawberries. For me and my mom, who was a student who got her Ph.D. in Anthropology, there were just so many contradictions that I had to face. Those things started a process for me, which was intensely introspective and questioning of everything around me. I feel kind of somewhere in between those worlds. There's this duality, because I'm constantly having to juggle between those two cultural experiences."

There were prejudices for the young De La Rocha to face and one experience in particular stood out during his high school years. During one lecture, a misguided quip from one teacher alerted Zack to the inbuilt racial prejudice some people exude without even questioning. De La Rocha would later explain to *Rolling Stone*, "He was describing one of the areas between San Diego and Oceanside, and as a reference to this particular area of the coastline, he said, 'You know, that wetback station there.'" This term is an ethic slur, commonly referring to Mexican immigrants who illegally entered the United States. It surmises that the illegal alien swam across the Rio Grande river which borders Mexico and Texas, as they entered the US, wetting their backs in the process.

"And everyone laughed," Zack continued. "They thought it was the funniest thing that they had ever heard. I remember sitting there about to explode. I realised that I was not one of these people, they were not my friends. And I remember internalising it, how silent I was. I remember how afraid I was to say anything."

From that point on, De La Rocha made a pact to himself he would not stand for this for the rest of his life like so many of his ethnic origin would often do. Zack kept his dignity at school and remained silent. The experience with his father had also grounded his emotions and he was a resilient, solitary figure. "I worry more just about what that experience did to me, how it affected my way of thinking," he later said, referring to the problems with his father. "I think it affected me in good ways too, because I feel like at this point what could anyone possibly do to me that could hurt me more?"

Beto himself has said (on www.aaa.si.edu) of Zack's unusual upbringing at his hands: "I don't regret it. It's a learning experience." He does however acknowledge that making his son fast because he was doing so was wrong. "He was too young for that," he reasoned. Still it seemed to surprise the elder De La Rocha that his son was even aware of the experience. "I only heard he had remembered this through other sources," Beto claims. "We've never talked about it. He'll come around when he's older, like I did."

Whether directly or otherwise, Beto De La Rocha's political stance and activities had a positive effect on Zack and he was determined to assimilate his own views with a goal of fundamental change. The seeds were growing even in a young teenager, proud of his roots and his Chicano way of life. Zack later referenced his father's beliefs and explained his earliest inspiration. "His attempts at trying to build bridges between the artists in Los Angeles, the workers, and Chicanos against Vietnam, led me, politically, towards the National Liberation movements," he told the *Nuevo Amanecer Press.* De La Rocha also credits his grandfather, who came from the Mexican state of Sinaloa, with some political influence, saying he was a revolutionary fighter. He migrated to America where he worked in agriculture, labouring in Silicon Valley, California.

"His working days lasted from fifteen to sixteen hours daily, sweating and subjected to poverty," Zack would explain, "I see his experience reflected in the testimonies of the Zapatistas, the indigenous peasant rebels who struggle every day to make a living." De La Rocha would later begin a crusade in support of the Zapatistas, much more of which is explained further in the book.

Beto De La Rocha perhaps also passed on the Mexican heritage now so prevalent in his son, through his other varying activities. He is said to have edited the United Farm Workers publication *El Macriado.* The UFW is a labour union formed in 1962, one that is still active today. Beto also helped reintroduce a Mexican celebration known as 'Day Of The Dead'. This traditional cultural event famously celebrates the lives of those living in the United States and Canada of Mexican heritage, after their death. This holiday was restored throughout America and these days goes far beyond, with celebrations noted as far as the Czech Republic and New Zealand.

Tom Morello and Zack De La Rocha were born from two disparate communities. Their upbringings were entirely different in many ways, though it's easy to see there were similarities too. Both were of mixed ethnicity in an era before political correctness helped change perceptions. Their respective parents were artistic, creative, intelligent and all fought for human rights, specifically the rights of their own peoples.

Though Kenya and Mexico are culturally and geographically far apart, the similarities in the struggles of their indigenous people were apparent. Likewise, the struggle for emancipation of all mixed race American residents of the Sixties and Seventies especially, is a uniting front with which De La Rocha and Morello had much in common. Oppression harbours the same negativity in any language or culture and the non-white races had long struggled with dictatorships, despite living in a supposed free land.

Their superficially polar upbringings therefore overlap

intriguingly despite being from different time periods and different locations. It was, you could say, fate that they would eventually meet. A clue to Zack De La Rocha's future path lay with a friend he made at high school in Irvine, a strapping older kid who was one of the cooler, more open-minded students at the school. The legend goes that Tim Commerford came across Zack one day in the school cafeteria and promptly taught him how to steal food there! Their school, 'University California Irvine Farm School' was a group of buildings that were formerly slaughterhouses of ranch-hands.

Tim Robert Commerford was born the youngest of five children, in Irvine on February 26, 1968. He was a lonely, isolated child in many ways and his family were wracked with tragedy while he was still attending high school. His mother, a mathematician and teacher, developed brain cancer when Tim was just seven years old and by the time he hit third grade a year later she couldn't understand or advise him on his school homework. Her husband, an aeronautics/space engineer, struggled with her illness and they eventually divorced, before he remarried. So Tim's cancer stricken mother had to move in with her sister in Sacramento, California all the while enduring intensive health care. Tim meanwhile, stayed in Irvine with his father, but their relationship was poor. "My job is to deal with my insecurities," Tim would later say. "I do worry about feeling good about myself. Before [RATM], there was a point where I didn't think that I was cut out for music. I nearly left it behind to be a carpenter."

At least he had De La Rocha, who would become a very strong, grounding influence in his life. It was he who introduced Tim to the bass guitar and inspired the gallant teenager to take up playing permanently, whilst also finding an emotional outlet in poetry, something he has continued ever since.

There was a long lasting bond formed between the two, and later in his career the bassist would speak of his enduring friend with affection, remembering their days growing up together. "When I first met him at his house he had this acoustic guitar and he taught me how to play the entire Sex Pistols album. He was breakin' at school when nobody else knew what hip-hop was. That kid was on it from day one."

Tragically Tim's mother would pass away from brain cancer in 1988. Tim would later develop an interest in tattoos and his first was a black band around his left arm to remember his mother by.

Chapter Three
In The Shadows

Despite the protestations of black America and his family's ongoing political prowess, Tom Morello was always destined for a life of duality as he entered puberty. On the one hand was the struggle between the varying races in the country and the fragmentary Vietnam war which so many protested and rallied against; on the other, was Kiss.

Most children of the Seventies have happy memories of growing up alongside the fire breathing, blood-dripping, four rocking horsemen of the Apocalypse known as Kiss. The merchandise branch of Gene Simmons and Co. incorporated everything from lunch boxes to gum wrappers. Kiss were a kids band. They represented rock stars but they were also comic book characters, fantasy idols. When Morello was growing up, Kiss were never without make-up and they therefore carried a level of mystique unique amongst rock groups. This was just one reason why they were the biggest band in the world.

"I loved Kiss," Morello would later tell *Raygun*. "I loved Midwestern 7-11 parking lot rock. That's what I was all about as a 13-year-old. That was coming from a very different place then, but the thing that I always found wanting in those songs, even as a young lad, was lyrical content. It was like, 'Well, this is a bunch of great riffs and I am being rocked by it, but it's about dragons and sorcerers!'"

Unlike future generations, the rock of Kiss was 'allowed' on public, mainstream US radio. In fact this was how most kids first heard the band. Kiss were great songwriters and with a wealth of catchy hook-filled rock they could appeal with any album, whether it be the good time 1974 era with the likes of 'Strutter' and 'Deuce', or the slightly later *Destroyer* material, which featured a plethora of fantasy rock 'n' roll verging on heavy metal. There was the Kiss theme 'Shout It Out Loud' and the nasty, spitting 'God Of Thunder', but *Destroyer* is most famous for the radio hit, 'Detroit Rock City' which had a riff to die for.

It was this song which steered Tom Morello towards a guitar for the first time. He went to the first teacher he could find and offered five dollars to be taught the mighty riff to either 'Detroit Rock City' or Led Zeppelin's 'Black Dog'. Yet he was stumped to be informed the guitar needed tuning first! Speaking to *Guitar World*, Morello would later remember, "I thought that was a huge waste of time when there were so many cool songs to be learned! But I tuned the guitar, and when I went back the next week, he said, 'Now we have to learn how to play a C major scale.' That was it, no more guitar lessons for me! I didn't play for four years."

That could have been that. As anyone who has learned guitar knows, the initial difficulties of getting used to the strings and frets can be off putting and you need determination just to play a chord, let alone a riff or a lick. Scales can also alienate creative types; it's the equivalent of learning algebra at school instead of sex education. Some guys, the innovators, just want to get out and play because they already possess the natural aptitude and are just aching to express themselves. This was Tom Morello. It would take a new type of sound to educate him to the possibility that scales and even tuning weren't always necessary.

Meanwhile in the UK, the country had been taken over by a contingent of belligerent and energised punks. They were led by the rowdy anarchy of the Sex Pistols whose *Nevermind The Bollocks ... Here's The Sex Pistols* was arguably the greatest punk album of all-time and contained such revolutionary gems as 'God Save The Queen', 'Anarchy In The UK' and 'Pretty Vacant'. It was quite unlike anything which had come before – or since. The focal point was singer Johnny Rotten, so called due to the poor state of his teeth. He had wide eyes (the result of a life-threatening bout of meningitis as a child) and a vocal delivery which you couldn't ignore. The cliché rang true: you either loved or hated this band. Most hated them, especially in conservative areas of their home country, and soon this aversion would spread to other countries as the Pistols built up a following of like-minded young anarchists in the making. Whether it was just to piss parents off or to actually engage in the deeper issues of the band's politics, this was the perfect anti-establishment band and best of all, anyone could play their stuff.

"I got the Sex Pistols record, and like so many other angst-filled, alienated suburbanites, I said, 'I can do that, too'," Morello would explain to *The Progressive*. "Prior to that, I was a big fan of heavy metal music, which involved extravagance. You had to have huge walls of Marshall amplifiers and expensive shiny Gibson Les Paul guitars. You had to know how to play 'Stairway To Heaven' and have a castle on a Scottish loch, limos, groupies, and things like that. All I had was a basement in Illinois. None of that was going to come together for me."

There was another musical troupe which would form the nucleus of young Tom's future and showed him it didn't have to be heavy metal fantasy to be a great musician. "I was in Europe when I was 19 years old, and I heard a record by Grandmaster Flash and the Furious Five in a record shop," he recalled to *Guitar One*. "It was the first time I had heard rap music. It was called 'Revival', and I immediately bought the 12-inch. That literally changed my life, and broke me out of the mould of white suburban rock. Until that, it had all been either punk rock or hard rock. I didn't really know that other kinds of music even existed. Sure, my mom had James Brown and Stevie Wonder records around the house, but I thought, 'Man, those don't really have kickin' guitar solos. That can't be music.' So that trip to the record shop was a huge change. Ever since, it's been important to me to incorporate that element into my music."

Grandmaster Flash and the Furious Five were arguably the first rap group, and they became a highly influential outfit, best known for their track 'White Lines (Don't Do It)'. In fact they were so significant in the history of music that in 2007 they became the first ever rap group to be inducted in the Rock 'N' Roll Hall Of Fame.

Tom Morello would leave Libertyville in his late teens when he was accepted at Harvard University in Cambridge, Massachusetts. Before this, however, he formed something of a joke group one day outside of drama class. The outfit would eventually feature childhood friend Adam Jones, who would go on to play guitar for Tool. Electric Sheep were a loose group of 'musicians' who mostly couldn't play. But nevertheless they showed potential by writing and playing their own material as opposed to cover songs. Even within their own school, Electric Sheep were something of an unknown quantity but those who were into the band were voracious supporters, turning up at all hours to witness garage rehearsals. Some songs known of today include 'She Eats Razors', 'Oh Jackie O' and 'Salvador Death Squad Blues', which hinted at Morello's burgeoning political beliefs. They did record one cover song however, Steppenwolf's 'Born To Be Wild' and it is the only known recording of the band to exist. It emerged from an LP titled *All Shook Up*, released by the school to showcase student talents.

"Adam wasn't in the original line-up," Morello would later explain. "There was this one guy who was sort of the principal player in the band – he was the only one in the group with any working knowledge of music, but he quit because he thought that he was far above us. Adam was his replacement."

It seems unusual today that Jones played four strings rather than six but he had previous experience, saying, "I played stand-up bass in the orchestra and I'd play bass with my brother, too. He'd play the guitar parts, and I'd play all the bass parts to Police songs or Fleetwood Mac or Chicago, or whatever he was into at the time. I was just so excited to officially be in a band. Of course, I had to borrow a bass because I didn't have one of my own. Electric Sheep had a pretty heavy rep in Libertyville. You know: terrible band, but great to see."

Morello would study political science and eventually gain an honours degree. In between lectures and his academic commitments, he pursued a relentless work ethic on guitar. Friends were actually worried about him, such was his dedication. It wasn't deemed healthy to be cooped up 24/7 either studying or practising guitar. But it was this commitment which set Tom Morello apart from his peers. He had a strong natural gift at the six strings but he would be the first to admit he was no Yngwie Malmsteen. Thus he was intelligent enough to realise that he had to work on his craft and develop a niche, his own way of expressing his unique creativity. This would eventually manifest itself in the scrapes, glitches and knob switchings so prevalent in Morello's future work: learning how a guitar worked, *really* worked. Not just pressing down the string on a fret to make the expected note, but wringing the life out of every potential high or low on the neck. Using every possible nook and cranny of a guitar to extort some sort of noise, as tuneless as it may have seemed sitting in a small room with a miniature amp. At times, inevitably it sounded downright awful, but Morello could hear the bigger picture, just what his apparent noise would sound like in the context of a band. A band which could fuse all his musical interests in one fell swoop.

He was an immensely hard worker. Most who attend establishments such as Harvard or Yale are of course intelligent and capable. But they tend to play hard to offset the intense work schedule of studying for a diploma. Morello was the opposite. When he had finished writing his thesis he would continue his studies on the guitar. Despite the concerns from those who were close to him, he knew it was nothing to worry about. It was his way of relaxing and deep down he did not want to be a political scientist or anything so corporate – he wanted to rock. The only way he would be able to achieve it was to practise until his fingers bled. The rock and metal scene of the Eighties was littered with such guys and girls who could play faster than the speed of light. Most of them were soulless cardboard cut-outs of other musicians of course, but the capability at wrecking a fretboard was never in doubt.

Every band needed a guitar wizard as its focal point and Morello already knew that to be successful he had to capitalise on his uniqueness and play up to that rather than trying to compete with the flooded market of fast but flunky guitarists. Equally, most musicians who moved to Los Angeles to compete in the 'big time' had ditched their jobs, if they had one at all. Therefore they could literally sit in their flea infested apartments and noodle away all day, perfecting their complex scales and techniques.

"I always thought that I was very much behind," Morello would later admit in *Guitar World*. "All of the guitar magazines described how Eddie Van Halen, Jimmy Page, or whoever, started when they were nine years old. I just felt that I was so far behind that I was going to have to work that much harder to catch up. Since I believe that I have no natural ability whatsoever, I had to fight for every single inch of guitar prowess. So when I was practicing for eight hours a day, for two hours I would just practice scales."

His routine was vehement and disciplined. He had bought a book called *The Guitar Hand Book* which he used to study guitar theory. Every day Morello would spend two hours studying theory, two hours trying to write songs and then another couple of hours experimenting with various noises through the guitar. "I began as the punk rock guitar player who refused to learn anything from anyone," he laughs today. "If you tried to show me a bar chord I would avert my eyes, like I would turn into a pillar of salt. And then I became waist deep in guitar excess hedonism, working up from two hours practicing a day to four to finally eight. And I'm not kidding when I said it was a disorder. I could have a fever of 102 and have an exam in the morning at Harvard and still have three hours to go, and I would do it. Many were concerned among my friends and family!"

Morello would later admit that he was a plagiarist in the beginning, though this is of course the quickest and best way to learn without formal lessons. From jazz guitarist Al Di Meola to Eddie Van Halen, Tom Morello developed a taste for trying to emulate each and every impressive guitar player and in doing so, built up a strong knowledge of various styles, all the while tuning his own ideas and inventions to impressive proportions.

Some influences stayed with him for longer than others, whether it be The Clash's Joe Strummer or, particularly, Gang Of Four's Andy Gill. "Gill had a huge influence on me," Morello told *Guitar One*, "He deconstructed the guitar in a way that really affected me and made me think. It sort of sounded like he was playing a different song than the rest of the band. When I first heard his playing I thought, 'That's awful.' Only later did I realise the genius in it."

Eventually Morello would become so adept at the rudimentary playing he would have no need to emulate anyone else and his practice routine would then involve him working on strange noises and new ways of bringing the best out of his instrument.

While still an intrepid novice, he happened upon the 'correct' way of doing things, it's just he didn't realise how or why. "I found I had stumbled on a lot of the things during my own hours of practicing that I was now able to put names to. The modes, for example. I puzzled out a lot of that before really knowing what it was, and how to relate them to keys and whatnot," Morello would say.

He would later expand upon his style, telling *Mad Stratter*, "Once you get off the beaten path of chords and notes, any noise can be its own microcosm of song writing. There is a deep library of songs that go from G to C. There is not a deep library of songs that use a toggle switch and a wah pedal. The possibilities are limitless with just those two things. Add an allen wrench that you use to bang on the strings and your options grow exponentially. I love that."

Morello originally had a Kay guitar, which was basically a cheap, department store instrument. It meant the strings were harder to hold down and in general it was more difficult to adjust to, but it was a good learning process for the young guitarist. If he could play one of these he could play anything. He saved some money and eventually bought a Gibson Explorer. "I got the Explorer just at the time when everybody was getting those 'Eddie Van Halen' Kramer one-knob guitars," he told *Guitar One*. "That was the cool guitar to have. And here I was, weighted down with this big chunk of wood that had all these volume and tone knobs. It was quite unhip. So I thought as long as I had the thing and it was paid for, I might as well find some application. So one day in my college dorm, I was messing around with the toggle switch and a wah–wah pedal. My roommate, my long-suffering roommate who had to endure my jamming for two years already, said 'Oh no, you bought a keyboard.' And of course it wasn't a keyboard. I had stumbled upon playing arpeggios with the toggle switch and wah–wah pedal. I thought perhaps I was on to something. That was sort of the first revelation that there were others ways to fiddle with the guitar." It was a disclosure, which would serve the young guitarist well.

By now Morello had relocated to Los Angeles himself, as he thought this was the place he had to be to gain rock stardom. "So

I moved there with no roots, no friends, just a list of names from the Harvard Alumni Association," he would explain. "Mom was wholly supportive of my decision. I moved out here with a thousand bucks in my pocket, which I spent on my first apartment on the corner of Normandie and Santa Monica Boulevard."

Morello had to find work once he had graduated and to tide him over while he pursued his real dream. Initially he hoped to find work as a substitute teacher, but had no luck in the Los Angeles School District. He had several jobs which he referred to as "soul crushing" but has not revealed their exact nature. One job became soul crushing for another reason and it was his most educational experience thus far. He landed a role as a scheduling secretary for Senator Alan Cranston, a Democratic Party politician and author.

"The Cranston job was a day gig, and it allowed me to rock in the evening," Morello would tell Jane Ganahl. "Oh, and he was one of the most progressive senators you could find issue-wise. As far left as you could be and still be electable. But it was also a very disconcerting experience. I got to see the internal workings of the political machinery and it was grim. He was a great man with all these ideals but spent all his time phoning up rich guys for money! Even when we would stop for gas."

Morello realised that even if the admirable Cranston were elected, he would still owe money to the corporations he so opposed. It was a vicious circle whereby in order to campaign against certain areas or organisations, Cranston needed their money in order to finance his own work.

Morello has said that he started working in the world of politics because it was the only decent job he could find, given his degree. He described his stint with Cranston as "a last-gasp attempt at parliamentary politics." And he recalled one particular incident which showed the level of indoctrinated prejudice he had to face.

"I had a woman ring up incensed because there were Mexicans moving into her neighbourhood," he told writer Ben Myers in his book of essays, *American Heretics: Rebel Voices In Music*. "I told her that it's far better to be living in a neighbourhood of Mexicans than a neighbourhood of loud-mouth racists. I thought I was doing good work for the senator but I got chewed-out all the way up and down the party line. They were pissed, you know? I thought that that was why I got into politics – to do the right thing – but it was painfully obvious that it just doesn't work that way. Any real substance of change – whether it's in workers' rights, civil rights or women's rights – will not come about from having rulers who sit around benevolently doling out gifts. It's their force to organise people at a grass roots level."

After two and a half years with Cranston, Tom Morello inadvertently found his boss in the midst of a financial scandal. He now had to find a new job but had certainly had enough of the official political environment. It seemed it was either music or nothing. But he was at a serious disadvantage: the 1980s were notorious for big hair, empty heads and glossy pop metal. To get in you had to look the part and that meant horrendous dress sense, teased bouffants and the obligatory cucumber down the trousers. This was not Tom Morello. He was mixed-race with short hair, who dressed like a relatively regular guy. He didn't express himself through outlandish clothes or actions, but in his words and beliefs. He had hoped to find like-minded musos with a grip on politics and perhaps a little anarchy.

What he found was a scene dedicated to the big rock videos on MTV, a desperate cesspool of the mildly talented and the strongly disillusional. The bands of the era were throwaway, shameless scourges on serious music and meaningful lyrics. Songs were about chicks, partying and going crazy. There was of course nothing wrong in such escapism, and Morello wanted to rock like everyone else. But dressing like a woman was not his idea of a ticket to the big time.

Bands like Poison looked like women, yet banged more 'chicks' than your average corrupt politician. And they had songs like 'Talk Dirty To Me' and 'I Want Action'. This was not the scene for a Harvard graduate. "I got to LA at the height of the glam era when Poison and Faster Pussycat were on top," Morello told *In Jersey Rocks*. "Because my hair wasn't long, and because of the colour of my skin, I couldn't get in a band to save my life! That resulted in years of frustration."

He also had an extra stylistic disadvantage, though it was largely self-imposed. Where everyone from Metallica to Guns N' Roses held their guitars as low down as humanly possible, just because you looked less of a geek the lower it hung, Tom Morello held his guitar virtually under his neck.

Partly because of the need to constantly play with switches and use every inch of the guitar to find his required sounds but also you feel partly out of a good natured rebellion against the 'norm', Tom Morello was the antithesis of the hard rock musician of the late Eighties. Yet he made a huge breakthrough when he found bands such as Fishbone and Jane's Addiction. Here were street-smart warriors with funky style and interesting, intelligent lyrics. In the case of both bands, their sound was utterly unique too. This was more like it. The crotch rock scene fell by the wayside as Morello gradually learned there was a smaller underbelly of like minded people within LA. Suddenly he found a pool of capable musicians who were open minded and equally desperate not to become a part of the hair scene.

So the rock scene was split into these two camps: the big hair party bands as against those in the alternative scene who still liked the sound of heavy guitars but didn't have to be sexist or plain dumb to express it. However, there were also few rock bands in either camp with black musicians. Perhaps the most prominent was the New York group Living Colour. Guitarist Vernon Reid had initially formed the Black Rock Coalition, an organisation which aimed to bring other black rock musicians together. It was through this service that he found numerous musicians who would join him on his crusade to establish a band he was determined to call Living Colour. Eventually he would settle on a stable line-up and the band would go on to become one of the best known proponents for the fusion of rock, soul and funk music. They would also inspire many other black musicians to form rock/metal groups, from 24-7 Spyz to The Hard Corps. With Living Colour's success, the major labels realised that suddenly even white kids were interested in black hard rock music, a revelation they'd previously avoided.

Such was the subliminal ignorance within the rock scene that when a black guitarist came along they were instantly thought to be the next Jimi Hendrix. After all, there had not been a more famous black guitar player, so every new six stringer had to face the indignity and irrationality of being compared to a one-off genius. It was an instant way for Tom Morello to switch off.

"I've always faced what I call the curse of the ghost of Jimi Hendrix," Morello would later quip. "People always ask me about him – in every single interview around the world. While I love and appreciate Hendrix, I've always totally, completely stayed away from any overt influence. Because no matter what style of music you play, no matter what kind of guitar player you are, if you have anything to do with rock and your skin is brown, some fool in the audience is going to yell for 'Foxy Lady' or shout, 'Play with your teeth'. So I intentionally shied away, and the reaction to me is very different now."

Morello had joined a soul/funk/rock band called Lock Up in the late Eighties. He replaced the original guitarist (who had actually formed the band). Mike Livingston, who was almost 20 years older than Morello, had been a quarterback in the National Football League for the Kansas City Chiefs. Perhaps given the success of Living Colour, the major labels were willing to take on the odd risk and Geffen records jumped all over Lock Up after a few local shows and a word of mouth reputation. Perhaps this was the next Living Colour …?

In a strange twist, future Rage Against The Machine drummer Brad Wilk would audition for Lock Up at one stage. Born in Portland, Oregon in 1968, Wilk grew up in Chicago before his family settled in southern California. At an early age Wilk grew accustomed to making and losing friends quickly as his itinerant father switched jobs with alarming frequency, from jeweller to bookmaker. "I try to live my life and find happiness in pretty basic things and not put a whole lot of emphasis on money either," his son would later say in *Raygun*. "That was everything to my father, and I saw it kind of ruin him. It made me really try and appreciate the things that don't cost money, which are the things that should be appreciated anyway."

The young Wilk – who is a Type 1 diabetic – also saw oppositions in his family's religious beliefs. While his father practised Judaism, his mother was a catholic. "Right there, that puts some questions in your mind," he told *Raygun*. "Contradictions. It just seems to me that the one thing that everyone had in common

– everyone I knew, anyway – with religions was fear. The fact of the matter is we have no idea where we came from. That's just the way it is, so it just kind of makes it irrelevant to me. When it came down to it, a lot of the reason why people would seek out religion was fear. And there just are no concrete answers."

Wilk failed to get the job with Lock Up. Still, there was a bond formed between Wilk and Morello and the guitarist would keep his new friend in the back of his mind for the future. Lock Up were a well known band amongst local musicians and a prominent fixture of the LA scene who attracted veteran musicians. The original drummer Michael Lee was to later play with Robert Plant and Jimmy Page, while his replacement was D.H. Peligro of Dead Kennedys fame. The band were to release their debut album in 1989, titled *Something Bitchin' This Way Comes*. Strangely considering his future endeavours, Morello's work on the album is closer to the standard of the times – lots of fast moving fret work and frenetic solos. There were however, the odd hints at his innovation, with the toggle switch friendly vibes of 'Punch Drunk' and 'Can't Stop The Bleeding'.

Something Bitchin' This Way Comes did no business for Geffen and in the aftermath of the apathy which met the album's release, Lock Up were dropped despite being signed to a two album deal. Morello would later add, "We asked about the second record and they said, in effect, 'Do you have the money to sue us?' And, of course, we didn't." It wasn't through Lock Up's own live shows that Morello experienced fame, but surreptitiously he stumbled upon an intriguing incident which showed him the bright lights of popularity.

In *Alternative Press*, he explained, "In 1989, [Jane's Addiction frontman] Perry Farrell asked us to impersonate Jane's Addiction at a New Year's show. So the lights would go off and they'd say, 'And please welcome Jane's Addiction!' and it would be my band, you know, me with a Dave Navarro wig, the singer with little braids, and we'd play 'Pigs In Zen'. So it was a joke on their audience, right? So, we stepped out on stage and it was dark enough so that the audience clearly thought that it was the band and I have never felt anything like the rush and the electricity. It was really like grabbing a live wire standing on that stage, from the incredible intensity. We did our little joke. They came out and finished the set and I walked offstage going, 'Man that is unbelievable.' I had never experienced anything like that onstage in my life."

The demise of Lock Up forced Morello's hand and proved a blessing in disguise. He could now form his own band with his choice of musicians, sound and outlook. His first port of call was Brad Wilk who by now was playing in a short-loved band called Greta. Ironically this group was also to experience the wrath of a major label. They released a pair of albums on Mercury Records before officially splitting in 1994 – at which point Wilk had long since left to join Morello.

Every story of the birth of a star or a whole group of stars is punctuated with decisive, fateful moments and first meetings. At this stage in the story of Tom Morello and RATM came just such an encounter. Conflicting reports suggest that on the advice of a friend Tom Morello travelled to Orange County, California, where he saw a far cooler alternative scene than the one in Los Angeles. Here was a hardcore/punk haven full of innovative musicians and inspiring poets and there he met a poetic vocalist. The other suggestion is Morello saw a performance in a Los Angeles club whereby he saw a singer he knew he had to work with.

Whichever story is true, it was at this point that Tom Morello met a young man named Zack De La Rocha.

Chapter Four
Ghost In The Machine

Like many kids who discover hardcore, Zack De La Rocha turned a corner when he fell upon this most uncompromising music and lifestyle. Simply put, it changed his life. Here was a movement which underlined everything he held dear – a positive view on changing your life and the society around you, one of strength, defiance, persistence, perseverance. These were the qualities he had needed growing up and suddenly a musical scene set alight all his thoughts and fears. The likes of Youth Of Today and Minor Threat permeated Zack's teenage years and he found himself gravitating towards the 'straight edge' lifestyle endorsed by these and other bands of the same ilk.

The lifestyle does not endorse drug or alcohol use of any kind. Some go further and even cut out caffeine and promiscuous sex. Additionally many straight edge practitioners follow a vegetarian or vegan diet. The term itself was coined by Minor Threat in their song 'Straight Edge', which inadvertently provided a blueprint for the scene that took its message literally.

De La Rocha had initially fumbled around with a guitar, even joining a band called Hard Stance where he played the six strings. But he soon combined his love of poetry and rap music to become a vocalist. Growing up he had been a fan of the rap culture and many artists from EPMD to Ice Cube. It was at a show of the latter that Zack realised the potential for his lyrics. Here was a huge star with the opportunity to say and do anything and people would listen. Zack decided that his hardcore sensibilities could easily be rapped, the way some Eighties hardcore bands almost already did. Youth Of Today singer Ray Cappo preached socio-political tolerance and would later become a Hare Krishna, defining the term Krishnacore with his post YOT band Shelter. De La Rocha's first band as a singer was called Inside Out and Cappo would remain instrumental in his early career.

Inside Out would release just one CD EP and a 7" single – *Spiritual Surrender* and 'Benefit' (a split live recording with Youth Of Today) respectively. Listening to *Spiritual Surrender*, it is amazing to hear the transition in the voice of the modern De La Rocha style. His early yelps were more in common with early Suicidal Tendencies and a Keith Morris-fronted Black Flag and showed no remote hint of his hip-hop prowess. The vocals were a strange mixture of melodic and impassioned singing (see the chorus for 'By A Thread') and the more typical shouting, gang style vocalising. Musically the band showed tremendous potential, with guitar and bass flourishes their peers simply did not possess.

Though they were often chaotic and seemingly unstructured, Inside Out's vitality and fury was undeniable. De La Rocha is deeper, huskier and more consistent in his vocals, there are far less dynamics at play than in his later Rage work. It's interesting to note the year of release is 1990, as this places the band squarely in between the classic early Eighties hardcore period where bands such as Minor Threat and Bad Brains ruled, to the latter half of the Nineties where hardcore became more emotional and experimental. Inside Out were a combination of all that came before and all that has since emerged and were fairly out of the loop in terms of 'right style, right time'. They had a fair helping of uniqueness, such as the emotive 'Sacrifice' which doesn't recall specific bands of any time period. It simply sounds like Inside Out.

"I believe in redemption," Zack announces convincingly on possibly the catchiest track, the band-penned 'Redemption'. Some argue that if the EP had benefited from a stronger recorded performance, then this band could have been one of the best known outfits of the hardcore scene, instead they were better remembered for their live performances, a fact illuminated by the failure of the CD to fully transfer that feral energy.

Part formed by hardcore legend Ray Cappo, Revelation Records would sign Inside Out on the strength of their incendiary live shows and frenetic material. When Cappo dismantled his band Youth Of Today and formed Shelter, he decided to take Inside Out on tour with them, beginning on June 15, 1990 at the Anthrax club in Norwalk, Connecticut. Bizarrely for a peace loving group, Shelter experienced protestors at the show, a bunch of atheist punks who distributed fliers for means of 'debate'.

It was time for Zack De La Rocha to make his first stand on a stage. During Inside Out's set, he held one of the fliers and remarked, "If anyone thinks that this swastika belongs on the same piece of paper as this Krishna symbol, you're all just fucking ignorant." Like all great musicians, Zack could back up his views and words with an explosive and breath-taking performance. He writhed and sprung around the stage screaming the words to the band's next song, 'Burning Fight'. Like Shelter, this was music *and* message.

"Whenever I used to listen to bands like Government Issue, Minor Threat or Scream," Zack would later say, "it always made me feel like I would just lose it if I had a microphone in my hand. It's such a healthy thing to get onstage and vent, especially in the hardcore scene. Anyone can just get up there and express themselves. Anyone."

Clearly De La Rocha did not feel he was a 'star' or anyone particularly special. In fact this viewpoint was part of his identification with the Zapatistas and indeed any people living in poverty. His was not a place to preach or lecture and he didn't feel as if he was any better than those in the audience just because he was a few feet higher up; rather, it was all just the means to an end. Inside Out would sadly not last too much longer when guitarist Vic DiCara decided to devote himself to being a full time Hare Krishna monk. Zack would attempt to keep the band active but the spark had gone and he knew he had to find a new muse. Inside Out disbanded in 1991.

Some time later, De La Rocha would look back on the band and state, "At that time I wasn't very active. I let my views be known but I didn't see the potential in music as a political weapon – a tool for direct action. Today we've been able to create an alternative media that reaches an enormous mount of people, instead of the usual media that misinforms people and only brings stories that serve the ruling class, instead of telling the population about what really happens."

He therefore knew that his next band could be the real deal – a tool for change and a chance to say the things that really needed to be said, the things we weren't told about on the daily news. He enlisted his old high school friend Tim Commerford (who had been playing high school football as a defensive end) and set about finding the right guitarist and drummer. He soon ran into Tom Morello and Brad Wilk, who just happened to be a Buddhist.

Like Morello, the latter had also grown up in the grip of hard rock heroes such as Kiss but unlike his new band mates he always knew the instrument he wanted to play. "When I was about 13 years old, in Chicago, a friend of mine who lived a couple of doors down had a Ludwig Silver Sparkle drum kit with a big Kiss logo on the front head," Wilk would later say. "I was totally infatuated with the drum set, period. So any time I could, I was on his kit, not knowing what the hell I was doing but banging away nonetheless."

Perhaps because of his octopi tendencies, Wilk was bound to be drawn to the one drummer who bounded with charisma and boyish charm, could hit like a volcano yet retained an unpredictable element to his playing: Keith Moon. The drummer with The Who first assaulted Wilk's ears on the landmark 1979 album *The Kids Are Alright*. "That record was a huge record for me," he told *DRUM!* magazine. "It came with that book inside, with all those amazing pictures, and they also had the movie as well. I was just fascinated by the energy and with The Who in general. The excitement that they were portraying as a band, I think that had a huge effect on me, definitely."

The Who were a rock 'n' roll band, and a damn good one, but that was only one style of drumming. For Wilk to advance his playing and develop the necessary chops for a serious band he needed some light and shade to his heavy type of tub thumping. His influence came in the form of Tower Of Power drummer David Garibaldi. He was ostensibly a funk/soul drummer but like the best, could turn his hand to any style. Rightfully he was acknowledged as one of the most influential sticksmen of his generation. Garibaldi used to run drum classes and here he met an eager 19-year-old Brad Wilk who sucked up the attitude of the great man and astutely learned the correct techniques.

"His nickname was 'The General,'" Wilk continued. "The guy was so intimidating, you saw it in his eyes: he had the confidence there. It was great. He had the confidence of knowing what he was doing. I love that fact that Keith Moon played with this unbelievable confidence, but he was on the edge of insanity. He was a driving force, but he was always just on the brink of completely losing his mind."

For Wilk there was a danger in being on the brink of missing a beat or not being fully able to play to the max. He needed to perfect his abilities and maintain strength of mind. During the six months that Wilk was under Garibaldi's tutelage, he learned to express himself in the way he had always wished, but with the assurance of knowing this time he was doing things the right way. He later explained to *DRUM!*, "Confidence to me is being able to get on a drum set and look at that drum set and know that you can pretty much play what you're thinking. You have a good sense musically of what's going on, and you feel confident as to what your abilities are. I'm not saying I always play like that! I beat myself up more than anybody could possibly do. I worry about just actually feeling good about what I'm doing. Anyone that's too confident may be selling themselves a little short. But if you're David Garibaldi, it's kind of like being the God of drumming. He's allowed."

Garibaldi pushed Wilk to further his own playing by entering the rhythm-driven realm of funk. Where he had previously stuck to the basic rock notions of powerhouse drumming, he suddenly realised that truly great drumming was as much about the space between the beat as the beat itself. "Garibaldi really taught me to focus on what's going on between the beats, the stuff that's kind of felt, less heard. Not necessarily space, but the feel of ghost notes, if you want to call them that. The feel in between the kick and the snare drum and where exactly you put that, really has everything to do with what makes you different from other drummers."

With the line-up for a revolutionary new band now in place, the quartet needed a name. They went with the title of an Inside Out album that never surfaced (it had also been mentioned in a 'zine called *No Answers*, written by DIY hardcore scene veteran and Ebullition Records owner Kent McClard, who was said to be friends with De La Rocha and Co.). It was a name that summed up their collective rhetoric and would give them a platform upon which to speak: Rage Against The Machine. It was a bold statement which spoke volumes, espousing the De La Rocha thought process that the callousness of the establishment was cold and inhumane. Something indeed to rage against.

Chapter Five
Freedom Of Speech, Just
Watch What You Say

April 29, 1992 was one of the most significant dates in modern political history. It didn't matter whether you were white or black; the injustice reverberated around the world. Four Los Angeles Police Department (LAPD) officers were acquitted of using excessive force in the beating of African-American cab driver Rodney King. The incident in which all four officers struck King several times while other officers stood and watched, was filmed and shown around the world in the aftermath. There were rumours, from the mainstream media amongst others, that King attacked the officers first and this was why they retaliated, yet the video doesn't show any force from King.

Surely there were enough officers in attendance to restrain him peacefully even if he were violent? That is what police training is supposed to be for. But black residents of Los Angeles, specifically the South Central area, were used to police brutality. Rap artists – most notably Ice T – had already been speaking of social injustices and police violence for many years. Most movies which highlighted the plight, even those which were brilliant reflections of the situation such as *Boyz N' The Hood*, were soft on the police element of the problems, instead focusing on the inter-gang warfare and personal battles. Many poverty stricken residents of inner city Los Angeles felt, however, that the police only exacerbated the fragile structure of daily life. It would soon become a cliché, but it was and continues to be very real for many living on the streets. To many, it seemed they were living in a police state, which the Dictionary Of Cultural Literacy defines thus, "A nation whose rulers maintain order and obedience by the threat of police or military force; one with a brutal, arbitrary government."

It was a bittersweet admonition to get such a brutal attack caught on tape but it awoke the rest of the nation and introduced the concept of the LAPD as a racist institution to the world. Then, when the four men who beat Rodney King were acquitted, LA reacted with complete anarchy. There were initially peaceful demonstrations at the verdict but gradually these were replaced by increasingly violent actions that saw attacks on whites and Latinos, police altercations and eventually the destruction of property, businesses and looting. This lasted several days and was an indication of the new age of media in which every move was being watched. The main news networks covered every inch of the rioting, as the world became a collective voyeur. Helicopter news crews hovered as the city went up in flames, innocent bystanders were attacked, stores were openly looted and rioters shot at police.

There were approximately 55 deaths and over 2,000 injured during the riots and the estimates of material damage varied between $800 million and $1 billion. There were over 3,000 fires caused which resulted in over 1,000 buildings being burned to ash and the fire department was on overload with a new call every minute at one stage. Roughly 10,000 people were arrested. "We sat in a hotel room in Calgary watching CNN thinking we should be there in the middle of it," Tom Morello told writer Ben Myers.

Was society becoming more violent, or was it merely being recorded more often? Something about the riots incited further bitterness amongst society, from the poor to the affluent. A look at the popular culture of the time outlines the new lust for blood. One of the biggest movies of the year was the film debut of Quentin Tarantino, the blood drenched gangster flick *Reservoir Dogs*. It was perhaps also ironic that the biopic of *Malcolm X* was released, starring Denzel Washington as Mr X. And though there was, in January 1993, to be a Democratic president, it seemed the future was as stark as ever.

But it was through music that society's ills were truly reflected as never before. Heavy metal was dying out in its present form with the advent of acts such as grunge lords Nirvana and Pearl Jam. Yet there was a newer, more feral type of musical aggression and that was the merger of metal with hardcore. Bands such as Biohazard, Madball and Sick Of It All had emanated from the classic NY hardcore scene of the Eighties, where the godfathers were Agnostic Front and Cro-Mags. The further development of the fast, aggressive sound was a lesson in tuning down guitars and upping the production values.

The most successful band to blend the hardcore, metal and even hip-hop elements was undoubtedly Biohazard. They had been active since the late Eighties and by the time of 1992's *Urban Discipline* album they had set a new tone in heavy rap over even heavier guitars. This was hardcore, metal, punk and hip-hop all at once and it was catchy as hell. Perhaps given their white ethnicity, Biohazard were not taken seriously as rap artists, despite the duel vocal talents of Evan Seinfeld and Billy Graziadei. This was music for white kids, perhaps even suburban white kids for the majority, which was ironic given Biohazard sang of inner city depravity, gang activity, poverty and every day social injustices. With the title track of their '92 opus for instance, the lyrics showed their outlook clearly, "The ways of urban life are not as they seem, standing up and fighting is what living here means. In order to survive you've got to earn your respect." Sick Of It All was another white band who combined harsh rapping skills over a blend of hardcore and a touch of metal but their appeal remained largely limited to the white suburban population.

What the music world needed to wake the slumber of the grunge mire and the metal preposterousness was a singer who would tell the truth but had the character and widespread street cred to appeal on a broader level. Step forward Ice T.

Tracey Marrow changed his name to Ice T in the early Eighties and began his rap career with tame beats and tales of women and parties. It was only when he decided to sing about his every day experiences that he started to develop a niche for telling the story of police brutality, gangsters, pimps and freedom of speech. Suddenly Ice T was big business and throughout the Eighties he would endorse his views with bigger and better music, including the seminal *Original Gangster* album, which featured one of his best and most famous tracks in 'New Jack Hustler'. It was on the 1991 opus where Ice finally gave a taste of the hardcore/metal band his fans had been hearing about. He debuted a track called 'Body Count' which sounded out of place on a straightforward rap album, but was a tantalising suggestion of where the music could go.

Ice T was by no means the first artist to experiment with rap over heavy guitars. Even Tom Morello's inspirational Clash had hinted at a possible new genre on their 1980 *Sandinista!* album with the likes of 'The Magnificent Seven', and 'Lightning Strikes (Not Once But Twice)'. But it wasn't until 1986 that the rap rock genre would receive its first real avocation with the merger of Run DMC and Aerosmith. Run DMC, a hip-hop trio from New York, took the riff from Aerosmith's landmark tune and rapped the lyrics. They even collaborated with the band for a truly memorable video.

1986 was also the year of a debut album by a band called the Beastie Boys – a white trio of rappers from New York and their snotty brash form of suburban nastiness featured a nod to the heaviness of the metal scene. On 'No Sleep Til Brooklyn' the group even enlisted the talents of Slayer guitarist Kerry King to play a solo.

Two years later one of the greatest hip-hop albums of all time hit the racks. Public Enemy's *It Takes A Nation Of Millions To Hold Us Back* was intelligent, witty, subversive and a damn fine musical collection. It contained a string of memorable numbers, from 'Don't Believe The Hype' to 'Bring The Noise'. It was also another opportunity for a black rap troupe to show their appreciation of heavy guitars. 'She Watch Channel Zero?!' again referenced Slayer, taking the riff from their legendary 'Angel Of Death' track. Then in 1991, Public Enemy would team up with thrash metal band Anthrax for an unprecedented world tour. The two also combined for one of the most famous rap metal tracks – a souped up version of 'Bring The Noise'.

But all of these rap metal pointers were simply moments in time where a flash of inspiration led to a sample or a one-off track. Not until Ice T's Body Count was rap metal truly shown in its full potential. The self-titled album was a rebellious romp through simple yet catchy riffs and hooks and an arsenal of revolutionary lyrics. Ice just took his straightforward rap lyrics one step further and, backed by a buoyant hum of dissident guitars and speedy drums, amplified his rebellion to the extreme. There were many highlights from the prison tale 'Bowels Of The Devil' to the heaviest track of the album, 'There Goes The Neighbourhood', which was a sarcastic stab at critics who wondered what on earth a full posse of black musicians was doing playing heavy rock.

There were sexy raps that Ice was well known for ('Evil Dick' and the hilarious 'KKK Bitch') and skits which were both ferocious and educational. How many white kids learned for the first time that there were more black males in prison than in college for instance? Unfortunately for Body Count, much of the genius of the album was lost in comparison to the closing track 'Cop Killer'. This was Ice T at his most confrontational and provocative and he probably knew there was going to be a hostile reaction to his lyrics, which is perhaps exactly why he wrote them.

The song predated the post-trial LA riots (though it did cite Rodney King) and as referenced earlier, mentioned the police brutality experienced daily by residents of South Central and beyond. Ice yells, "My adrenaline's pumpin', I got my stereo bumpin', I'm 'bout to kill me somethin', A pig stopped me for nuthin'!" And the chorus was simple yet effective: "Cop killer, better you than me, cop killer, fuck police brutality! Cop killer, I know your family's grievin' (fuck 'em), cop killer, but tonight we get even."

The song caused outrage within the conservative establishment, including usual suspects. Tipper Gore, founder of the right-wing organisation PMRC (more of which below) and US Vice President Dan Quayle were widely outspoken about the 'dangers' of such artists and their lyrics. Some politicians were brave enough to defend the right to freedom of speech but their words went largely suppressed and unheard. Quayle branded the song 'obscene' and even the then President George H.W. Bush waded in, criticising the record company for releasing such a song. Several stores were then forced to remove the album from sale after threats from the government screened through local law enforcement. In one store in North Carolina, the management were told that police would not respond to any emergency calls at the store unless they removed the album from the racks. Later, executives of Body Count's label Warner Bros (not exactly the most subversive establishment in general) received death threats and shareholders threatened to remove their funding unless the album was withdrawn. On his own terms, Ice T decided to cut the track, now it had caused maximum offence but had started to detract from the music and other messages. The album was then reissued with an ironic track called 'Freedom Of Speech' in its place. This was an already existing Ice T track from his 1989 album *The Iceberg/Freedom of Speech … Just Watch What You Say* but was modernised and appended appropriately. The full lyrics are recommended reading but, in particular, the insight into the art of censorship was priceless, including a reference to Tipper Gore.

The Parents Music Resource Center (PMRC) was formed by Al Gore's wife Tipper and several other wives of powerful political figures in 1985. They became known as the 'Washington Wives' and their intent was "to educate and inform parents" about "the growing trend in music towards lyrics that are sexually explicit, excessively violent, or glorify the use of drugs and alcohol" (though alcohol was of course taxed and available on every street corner throughout the United States). To this end they introduced the concept of the Parental Advisory warning sticker which would be placed on the front of any album which featured so called 'explicit' lyrics. This meant anything from swear words to sexual or violent lyrics. It was the musical equivalent of ratings for movies, the difference being there was no rhyme or reason. Anything remotely incendiary or ambiguous was instantly labelled as unsuitable and thus worthy of a sticker.

The truth was, if a parent was caring and interested in their child's life and social activities they would take a keen interest in their listening habits anyway – they didn't need a sticker to tell them to read the lyrics first. Additionally if they were an integral part of their child's every day existence, they would be the first to explain a particular set of lyrics, regardless of their content. There were no attempts at age ratings for music, it was simply a way of the establishment marking any record they felt was potentially dangerous, not to the youth, but to their system. Of course, as Ice

T and many others remarked, the stickers only served to draw attention to the records rather than divert it. And for all those parents who took no interest in their children's lives, they were still none the wiser to the mounting piles of potentially dangerous albums and lyrics.

The PMRC began as a reaction to certain pop artists' lyrics – most notably Prince and Madonna, for their 'suggestive' sexual words and actions. But they soon opened up an entirely unexpected can of worms when they started to research the heavier reaches of music. They then proceeded to incite the wrath of the entire heavy metal community by attempting to outlaw recordings by everyone from Judas Priest to Mötley Crüe. Some alleged threats to the safety of minors were perhaps more understandable than others. Where the PMRC referenced the 'occult' lyrics of satanic metal band Mercyful Fate and the aggressive sexuality of W.A.S.P.'s 'Animal (Fuck Like A Beast)' there was possibly an argument for an explanation to the youth. Yet they went too far by citing ridiculously tame bands such as Def Leppard and Twisted Sister for their 'unsafe' lyrics and this was where the musical congregation rebelled.

Besides it wasn't the point that some records were deserving of censorship and others were not. After all, who would decide which lyrics were suitable? It would be the PMRC themselves of course. Therefore every right-minded person and freedom fighter had to argue the merits of anything and everything being allowed. Over the ensuing years, many bands were guilty of trying to outdo what came before them with increasingly violent, misogynistic lyrics, most likely in an attempt to stir controversy and increase record sales, which often happened.

In 1987, as a reaction to the onset of the PMRC, Tom Morello's mother Mary – who is, remember, part-Irish and part-Italian – formed her own coalition, the anti-censorship brigade Parents For Rock And Rap. She left her teaching job of 22 years in order to speak out on the issue of censorship.

"PFR&R is a watchdog for artistic freedom in the music industry," she said on the official website. "It will monitor legislation and work to expose and combat all forms of music censorship. It came about as a result of my extensive research of the

PMRC. There seems to be a need to counter some of the measures they use to suppress artistic freedom. It was a result of biased coverage of rock and rap in some of the press. Thirdly, from the material that I read, I realised there were many parents who supported the First Amendment right to artistic freedom and this silent majority needed to be brought together to be heard." Still as vocal and energised as ever.

She would tell interviewer Kevin Johnson, "I think it's a person's prerogative to speak the way they want. There must be lots of comics in nightclubs who speak similarly and they don't get harassed. I think it might be partly a racial thing and I've always fought for racial justice." She even added that her son Tom was a hard rock musician but also a "nice boy", adding, "You can't hide the world from young people. You give them a good ethical base for surviving and living. Then they choose and you support them."

Mary Morello set out the following pointers for the goals she wanted to achieve with PFR&R:

1. To have a centre for a network where people can be reached to put pressure on governments on the local, state and federal level who attempt to take freedom away from artists.

2. To respond en masse to other types of organisations bent on censoring or eliminating works of art.

3. To boycott corporate and other organisations disposed to back those who censor or who themselves censor.

She also asked people to contact the centre, "When you hear, read or see evidence of the above," and "the network will reach out to help pressure the organization to back off from their attempted suppression of artistic freedom."

Ultimately the likes of moralistic groups such as the PMRC were about control and suppression of the general population, a division of the government and an attempt to push society down to the point where it had no way to affect change, and no way to communicate or self-educate. As Ice T told Mike Heck, "Tipper Gore was like the conservative family values person where the

Democrats could say, 'Well we're family values, we got Tipper.' I think that what she does now will be more covert. In other words, you won't see her speak; you'll just see actions coming out of the White House. I don't think she'll be out rabble rousing and doing her thing anymore. We'll just see more actions. So people have to start realising that we have to get more into print and our own underground ways of communication. If they determine that the people are talking too much with each other and starting to understand each other, they're going to cut communication off." He was absolutely right.

The likes of Ice T and Mary Morello managed to stem the flow of organisations such as the PMRC and, as the former suggested, Tipper Gore did indeed take herself out of the limelight and ceased to campaign so fervently, instead making odd comments in interviews and writing sickly sweet 'American Values' books. The damage had been done however.

Ice T certainly does not always get the credit he deserves for the rap metal movement. Without him the genre would have been very different and may not even have come along in quite the same way (Rage Against The Machine were even later given their first major tour support slot with Body Count in 1992, so it's clear they were approving of the career and views of Ice T). There may have been more to it as well. Remember the initial Body Count, self-titled track from 1991? The lyrics concerned the struggles of young inner city black males and the chorus was a refrain of, "Tell us what to do ... fuck you!" It's remarkably similar in intent to a line RATM would use to great effect a year later.

It wasn't just Ice T. The Clash with their pre-hip-hop rapping, Public Enemy with their subversive and innovative take on rap, with a hint of metal and the other incidental movements within the history of rap/rock – all these things combined to influence, inspire or just give background to the direction that the early Rage Against The Machine would take. It would eventually become a dirty term but in the early Nineties the sound of rap and metal combining was an exciting prospect. Until now, no one had combined it to any great degree other than Body Count. But there was going to be one rude awakening for the advocates of censorship and a rallying cry for the people against it. 1992 was a tumultuous year but it was one that fuelled the anger and attacking bite of ten tracks of political rhetoric. It was time to rage against the system.

Chapter Six
Preparing The Message

The musical merging of Messrs De La Rocha, Morello, Commerford and Wilk was an instant success. Most bands struggle to get a grip on their combined talents when they first jam together. The bassist and drummer lock into a rhythm but the guitar player can't find the right notes to accompany them. The singer has a batch of incendiary lyrics, which he's desperate to voice yet the music lacks a spark or the right backing for him to hit the notes. Maybe the guitarist is brilliant but the drummer can't keep time. Maybe, like most bands, it just *wasn't* meant to be.

With Rage Against The Machine, it was undoubtedly meant to be. What were the chances of Morello and De La Rocha meeting, having been born on opposite sides of the country and experienced two vastly different (yet strangely similar) childhoods? What were the odds of De La Rocha and Commerford being a pair already and Morello and Wilk separately uniting before all four together? Perhaps great bands are not born – they are found. Perhaps they are born out of chemistry.

"The only thing that is certain is the unpredictable nature of things," Tom Morello later acknowledged. "You never can predict the most important things. You could have gotten all the music industry heads together and not come up with a Jane's Addiction, for instance. But somewhere brewing in some basement or attic is going to be something as startling and as great as a Jane's Addiction or a Nirvana or a Clash or a Public Enemy. Those bands don't come out of some planning session, they come out of some musician's imagination."

Morello proved he had no talent for clairvoyance and surprised even himself with the eventual interest in the band. "Because the band was so radically different from anyone else, we had no ambition to even play a show," he told Ben Myers. "There were greater barriers then. We were an inter-racial band – a black guy, a Chicano guy, a half-Jewish guy … that was rare. Combined with the Marxist polemic and this new rap-rock hybrid, there was nowhere for us to play."

Within a few weeks of forming, the newly christened RATM had several songs together, including the future show stormer 'Bullet In The Head'. This was no average connection; it wasn't something Morello could have achieved in Lock Up, nor De La Rocha in Inside Out. Those bands were different entities and both had potential but they were never likely to manifest beyond a small rehearsal space. For this particular pair of musicians to find success and their ultimate niche, they needed each other. This was less about a personal friendship, and more about a common goal. Like all the best combinations of singer and guitar player, there was a slight aloofness between the two. You were never likely to see Morello joining De La Rocha on the mike with his head on the singer's shoulder in admiration, but there was a bond, which was strong enough to make this a real unit. It was two sets of friends coming together, and each pair was essentially closer to their first pal.

"With the first record, we wrote most of those songs during the first month we knew each other," Morello would explain in *Kerrang!*. "Zack had a book of poetry and lyrics, and we just bashed those out in the first rehearsals." Though the self-titled album would eventually contain just 10 tracks, the band actually wrote 15. These came together effortlessly, which given the intensity and volatility of the material was *remarkable*.

Tim Commerford would expand upon the recording process sometime later, saying, "We write the music before. We're riff-rock without question. We get together, come up with riffs, hook them with other riffs we've done, and then arrange the songs. We'll hear the vocals most times, and the chorus, and then we give the songs to Zack to be able to spend time to write the words. When someone brings in a riff, or we arrange a song, me, Brad and Tom can go home, work on it, and get better at it right then and there, whereas Zack has to go and hash out the words and he can't work on it until he gets the words done, so that takes some time."

To begin with, Zack free-styled over the music to get a feel for where the words would go. Once the vocalist had the lyrics in place, he set about rapping them with as much ferocity as he could muster. When it first happened, the band was both surprised and thankful to have someone of De La Rocha's calibre fronting them. The rolls, yelps and anger of future live shows was already part of the band's show, even as far back as the first rehearsal.

"Zack was doing that in our first rehearsal together," Morello would say of his singer's fiery stage presence. "Like, when we were just writing these songs. I remember there was a fateful day where I think we were writing the song 'Township Rebellion' and, up to that point, Zack had just been rapping. There had been none of the sort of hollering parts." As Inside Out had been more in line with the precision shouting Zack would become famous for, his old friend Tim suggested he start to infuse the song with a little more of that fire. "He did this just terrifyingly beautiful yell," Morello said, "and since then, that became an integral part of expression during the songs."

It was now time for Tom Morello to fully realise his expertise at creating unusual and inspirational noises from his guitar. He would later acknowledge that one of his prime early roles was to double as a DJ, given the band's strong hip-hop influence. He would listen to local hip-hop radio station KDAY and take note of the noises made by DJs. Remember, this was a kid who was predominantly used to rock music and the surprise elements of his guitar playing were unique to him. He had never had to put them into the context of a real band and he'd never quite been so inundated by hip-hop as when he met Zack De La Rocha.

Morello would state that hearing noises from DJs and trying to convert them to guitar "really took my playing to another realm. The toggle switch now became like a DJ's kill switch. I started thinking about the guitar in an entirely different way. I didn't look at it as a way to apply music theory to chords, notes, and scales. I looked at it as a piece of wood with six wires and a few electronics that could be manipulated in a much wider variety of ways. And then I used it not as just the icing on the cake, but as the whole meal. I began to try to craft songs out of the noises and textures."

For Rage Against The Machine, it all began with the live show. It's a cliché which most bands spout in unconvincing fashion, 'Live is what we're really about'. RATM were especially always about much more than just an hour on stage but their live show defined them. If you wanted to know what they were about you just had to witness them tearing it up on stage. And their performances were never less than outstanding. They didn't do weak shows or ever give less than 100%. Commerford and Wilk were always phenomenally tight, Morello never skipped a note and De La Rocha was a livewire, bounding around the stage with unlimited energy but capable to stop and enunciate his words clearly when he needed to make a vital point.

Very quickly it became apparent that there were few, if any, live bands around who could touch Rage Against The Machine, certainly no one of their era. Sure there were decent live acts and plenty of bands could replicate their studio output note for note which was an impressive feat. But this was beyond mere reproduction; it was about each song taking on a new life night after night. No song was ever the same twice yet every time they were somehow flawless, passionate and meaningful. It was indeed a brave band who took RATM out on the road with them, and many bands were soon to realise this.

Though the band first played at a friend's house party in Orange Country to get a feel for how their material would translate to an audience, their debut show proper was at the Jabberjaw club in Los Angeles in 1991. It had taken three months of rehearsals and tightening but the band were ready. There are usually glitches in every new band's first performance but it was hard to find one here. The audience were spellbound and word spread quickly that this band was clearly above the norm: they had only been together a matter of months, and they were already playing like *that*!?

"The crowd reaction was so intense that it was a big celebration of frustration and anger," Morello said of the band's debut. "It was a remarkable feeling. I realised that we had something special and that maybe we could take this thing further."

Brad Wilk concurred, later telling Ben Myers, "It was a pretty amazing show and it's still one of the highlights of our career. What we did was rehearse for about three months, consciously said 'Fuck the record companies' and instead put a tape together to sell at shows, although to be honest we really had no idea that any record company would even be interested in a band like us. But at that first show, the reaction from the crowd was so intense and so right on with what we were portraying that it was one big communal celebration of frustration and anger. It was a remarkable feeling for a debut show. It was afterwards that I realised that we had something special, whereas beforehand I hadn't been completely sure. I guess I realised the effect that we could have on an audience. That feeling never goes. I love it."

The band had been organised enough to produce that tape in readiness for their performance, perhaps sensing that once people saw the show they would instantly want to hear their material again and again. With no record company support and no previous experience, the members of Rage produced a full 12-song cassette, part-demo part-finished album. There was an immediate political statement whereby the cover of the tape featured a photo of the stock market and there was a single match taped to the inlay card, the message being: fuck the system, burn it down.

Many of the songs would be used for the full debut album; the likes of 'Bullet In The Head' were already well established. In fact this particular version was left exactly as it had been on the demo, such was its ferocity. There were other tracks however which the band ultimately felt were not strong enough. Though there was one particularly strong track left behind, the compelling 'Darkness Of Greed', other songs were less noticeable by their absence; 'Auto Logic', 'The Narrows', and 'Mindset's A Threat' among them. Still, the band managed to sell 5,000 copies of their self-produced album which was no mean feat. And it led to immediate record company interest. If a band could fire out 5,000 tapes on their own merits and draw the crowds, there had to be some financial potential here.

Morello was adamant his new band would not follow the route of Lock Up, nor did he want to make a habit of financing his own records *a la* Fugazi and Dischord Records. He knew there was massive potential in the band and that he would need a major label in order to truly get the Rage message to the masses. But under no circumstances was he to relinquish control. He would read the very finest print of any contract the band would be offered and would insist the band had full creative control. He had been young in Lock Up and equally he was not the leader of the band so he had less say in the decisions they made. With Rage, however, he ultimately knew what was best.

Morello would later explain his theory behind the music business, which was intellectual and revelatory. He told *Times Pop* critic Robert Hilburn, "I've come to think of the music business as this layer of people – the managers, the attorneys, the record company executives – who are like the landlords of this building that is the music industry. Whether we are talking about the Eighties or the Nineties, the bands just rent a room for a short time. These landlords all know one another and have business dealings with each other, long before you put your band together and long after your band is dropped from the label. Their interest is more in keeping the building in good shape than in the interest of the people who check in and out. When you are fortunate enough to be in a band as successful as Rage Against the Machine, you get to rent the penthouse suite, but only for as long as you are able to sell records."

This was not merely a future revelation; Morello already understood the inner machinations of the industry at the inception of RATM. Yet, once one understands the system, one can exploit it. "The important thing is to know what you are up against," he would also say. Rage, by their own admission, were lucky in the sense that some of their first shows were in support of an extremely popular local band formed by Morello's old friend Adam Jones – Tool. It only took two shows playing packed houses with the art rock band for Rage to be offered a deal with a major label. Several labels showed interest but also demonstrated their lack of understanding about what they could "do" with such a band. Great energy, great riffs, but where do they fit? How can we sell this?

Epic Records however showed an impressive grasp of the Rage style and seemed to know exactly how to market them. "They really seemed to understand where we're coming from," Morello remarked, "and they were willing to put in writing that we had 100% creative control over every aspect of our careers, which was paramount to us. Once that was out of the way, then I had no argument with being on a major."

Epic were certainly major. Initially launched by the CBS Corporation in the Fifties as a jazz and classical label, they were taken over by Sony in the Eighties. Over the years, Epic had been responsible for the success of The Clash (something which probably didn't go unnoticed by Tom Morello), Michael Jackson, Ozzy Osbourne and Meat Loaf. It did seem to go against the ethics of the band to sign with a major label, one of the fiercest forms of corporation in the material world. Yet the deal they negotiated was nothing short of remarkable. RATM insisted they would get to make a guaranteed three albums. If Epic did pull out after the first album, they would have to pay the band an extortionate sum. This wasn't just common sense, it was imperious business practise, the kind top attorneys in New York City would charge $1000 an hour for. At the time Rage were signed, one of Epic's biggest bands were grunge superstars Pearl Jam who had released their classic *Ten* album in 1991. Epic's representative Michael Goldstone, who signed RATM, was also responsible for Pearl Jam, and assured Morello and Co. that Rage was just as important. They knew they were onto something.

Still, Epic probably didn't expect too much from the band. It's not in a major label's interests or psyche to be hopeful; they generally cover the losses before they even start. Likewise Rage might even have given them a blessing by insisting on three albums because if the first flopped they'd have another two chances to make their advance back. Rage themselves were not overly optimistic about their sales potential, despite having sold out of their own cassettes. This was major leap to a major label and what if that 5,000 were the only ones who were interested? It was also not difficult to see irony in a huge corporate establishment willing to support a band with such revolutionary, anti-corporate lyrics.

This was a band who couldn't avoid being political especially now there was a tandem of freedom advocates with Morello and De La Rocha. Many would assume that because the latter wrote the lyrics, these were only his views but Morello was such a stickler for running the band that he wouldn't possibly endorse any views he didn't agree with himself, or at least empathise with.

In the future, Zack would write about the Zapatistas which was not exactly a chief concern for Tom Morello but the guitarist still backed the sentiments. And remember, his father had been heavily integrated in African politics.

"There was a political atmosphere in my home that I took for granted," Morello has said of his early life. "We had pictures of Jomo Kenyatta and Kwame Nkrumah [first President of Ghana] up in the house. When I got to high school and started studying world history and US history, I heard a different perspective on world events and that made me challenge a lot of things." What Morello was referring to is the false version high school kids are given of history, especially in the US.

Rage Against The Machine would eventually be heavily criticised for espousing certain views that seemed to oppose the ideals of being on a major label. Yet the integration of their art and politics would always crossover whether they liked it or not, so they decided they may as well use the system to their own advantage and spread their views as widely as possible. In hindsight they can be shown to have done exactly the right thing, and not just because they went on to sell millions of records.

Yes, in hindsight, Tom Morello was utterly justified in signing to a major label when he did. Sure, Rage might have developed an even bigger reputation and been able to sell their own material, perhaps even around the world. But ultimately their words would have been heard by only a tenth of the people they could reach through the distribution offered by Epic. Best of all, RATM were advocates of freedom of speech and spoke about real issues which affected society – Zack's lyrics were intelligent, subversive and could incite insurgency.

"Political activity and standing up for your rights are every much a part of human history as broken hearts and driving around in cars during the summer, about which there have been a great many songs written," Morello would tell www.morphizm.com. "Music can be a tremendously inspirational tool for agitation and organization. I know it has been for me and I feel that some of the music I've been involved with in the past has done that for other people. So it would be foolish for someone to argue that politics and art shouldn't mix. Escapist music is very political in upholding the status quo. That culture shapes the social landscape and makes certain things are okay. You may not hate gay people, but if ten of your favourite rap artists are constantly singing homophobic songs, it contributes to an atmosphere in which it's okay to dislike gay people. So in that sense all music is political."

One of the best things about Rage was their lack of arrogance, soulless lectures or superiority. They were not saying they were better than anyone else for knowing the things they did and they were not claiming to be all knowing. They simply put their lyrics out there for people to learn about and make their own interpretations and discoveries. For instance, drummer Brad Wilk would admit in *Raygun* that, "before I was in this band, I was kind of in the same boat as a lot of people. Not necessarily sedated by the media, but I didn't know of any outside sources of information. And my eyes have been opened a great deal. But it's hard for me to sit here and say that I'm as politically motivated as, say, Tom would be, 'cause I'm not. I think what we're doing as far as just opening people's eyes is definitely important, and I think it goes hand in hand with the music."

RATM were making a statement with more than just their explosive music. The first batch of T-shirts the band made featured instructions for producing a Molotov cocktail as the back print. Lifted direct from *The Anarchist Cookbook*, the image did not provoke the reaction the band had possibly expected. It was only in France where they felt they were going to be in trouble with the authorities, so they made their way out of the country fast. But they had set their stall out, Morello cracking, "I think that kind of thing is important. If people are not checking *The Anarchist Cookbook* out of the library anymore, they can always look at the back of a Rage Against The Machine T-shirt the next time civil disorder breaks out in the neighbourhood."

Chapter Seven
The First Manifesto

It is impossible to overstate the impact and genius of Rage Against The Machine's eponymous debut album. Exciting, innovative, rallying and utterly fantastic musically, the record pulsed with an energy few, if any, could match. Quite simply nothing like this had been heard before. As we have seen there were elements of metal in rap and vice versa. Not until Rage came along did the genre receive its first and chief advocate. The guitars sounded fantastic, heavy as a sledgehammer and funky to boot. The rhythms were choppy and bathed in soul, whilst the vocals were of another world. Here was a soulful lyrical poet who could shout with the best of them. It wasn't a part of the rap scene to shout; that was more a metal thing. Rappers tended to be smooth, because every word had to be heard clearly. The roughness wouldn't generally have transcended to a chopped up beat. With metal, however, the ability to sound gravel-voiced and angry was positively welcomed. In fact, metal had to be harsh and angry. So here we had harsh, angry rap placed over a grooving rock beast which swayed and moved with a host of clever dynamics. Today, rap rock is de rigeur but in 1992 it was a new entity. The instantaneousness of hip-hop, where words were drilled direct and quick to the brain and the brutality and groove of the metal scene was a marvellous combination. The album still sounds fresh and alive and will possibly never date but especially in '92, this was some funky shit and it rightly tore the music world a new backside.

Everything about the band was unique. There were cascading rhythms which didn't have the right to be on the same page, let alone during the same song. Vocal prowess which had never been heard before – the vicious rapping, the guttural admonishments and the lyrical beauty and effectiveness. And Tom Morello's self-taught school of chief DJ had brought new depth to his playing. Thus the band were proud to declare "No samples, keyboards or synthesizers used in the making of this recording." For my part, I don't mind admitting when I first heard some of the tracks, I was convinced there were umpteen members and various samples, DJs and other hip-hop accessories. I read the disclaimer and couldn't quite believe it, perhaps even wondering if it were true. Then I saw the band live and realised everything could be faithfully recreated. No doubt about it, Tom Morello *was* a visionary.

He would later clarify: "The reason why we did the 'we don't use samples' etc., was not out of some militant anti-sampling stance, it was because we, through our band's unique chemistry, were able to generate a lot of really off-the-wall sounds and textures using a punk rock line-up. And we wanted you to know that what you were hearing, we were just kind of making it, standing in a room plugged in."

For the collective RATM genius, the others needed to offer their own expertise. To feature such soulful playing of the rhythm section was a divine gift. There were unusual elements in both drum and bass – the latter played a prominent part in the overall sound, sometimes carrying the entire song whilst Morello played quirky noises over the top, as on the verse of 'Bullet In The Head'. This was unusual in a rock band, as many groups of that ilk featured two guitarists, one of which played a rhythm along with the bass. Even if there was only one six stringer, he usually stapled his rhythms throughout the song, leaving little room for the bass to breathe. Only a few unique acts like Pantera can be cited to be any different. They would leave the one guitar of Dimebag Darrell to take centre stage when required and only play the solo, leaving the bass to emphasise the rhythm.

Certainly, the prominence of the bass guitar in Rage's manifesto was more in keeping with the roots of rap and, to some extent, reggae. The one constant riff or backing track carried the song and vocals simply added to the effect, taking centre stage. With Rage the difference, and overwhelming selling factor was, the guitars came in when required to make a pounding dynamic. You could reduce every song on the album to a straightforward rap number, with no histrionics or yells and still, lyrically at least, it would be challenging and impressive. The essence of the RATM song is the hip-hop beat and the thumping bass, with the De La Rocha vocal delivery. This would be more than enough for most basic rap songs. Yet their secret weapon was undoubtedly the addition of the guitar background noises and most importantly the sections where the guitar took centre stage for a driving riff or to kick in for a powerful chorus.

Lyrically the album follows a similar pattern yet has numerous differences, which make each track unique. In truth, Zack could have been singing about buying a pint of milk, if he delivered the same vocal style and passion the music would still have sounded amazing. But because of the words one could pick out, because of the words you could read in the lyric sheet, the whole record suddenly took on a whole 'nother dynamic. This was *powerful*.

"I try to place myself in settings in which the environment around me is conducive to trying to create a more realistic picture of what it is like to live in America," Zack told Ben Myers regarding his lyrical approach. "What the American experience really is. Also I try to write about some of the experiences outside of America. On the last album I tried to raise the volume of voices of people who are trying to fight for their own liberation, which to me is the essence of what I do as a poet; I try to take my own experience as well as other people's and make them tangible through song. I think there's a distinct difference between artists that talk about politics and artists who directly experience something and allow it to filter into the poetry of whatever it is they are writing about."

Rage Against The Machine was produced by Garth Richardson (son of legendary producer Jack Richardson), better known as GGGarth. The Canadian is legendary within hardcore and alternative circles and produced a host of great underground albums during the Nineties, including records by the likes of L7, Melvins, Shihad and Testament. More recently he has presided over recordings of Biffy Clyro (*Puzzle*) and Bloodsimple's *A Cruel World*. I spoke to him directly about his role with the first RATM album, firstly asking him to explain how he became involved with the band and the album.

"I was working with Michael Wagener as his engineer; he was doing a mix for Michael Goldstone," he explains. "Michael Goldstone asks Michael Wagener whom he should get to produce the Rage record. He says Garth Richardson. I met with Michael Goldstone in LA. He played me the demos. I was blown away. We set up a meeting with the band and they played me three songs. After my jaw was picked up off the floor we talked for a while. Zack was laughing about my stutter through the whole meeting. That is why I go by GGGarth. A lot of people don't know how to handle my stutter. I go by it so they see I have a good laugh about it."

As for his role in overseeing the album, GGGarth says, "My job as a producer on this record was to capture this band as a band. I came up with the idea of setting up a PA in the live room and putting Tom and Tim's amp in outside rooms and then feed everything back through the PA. Brad had to wear headphones. He was sitting behind the PA so the bleed would not be too bad."

The basic songs as they were already written were mostly left untouched, though as GGGarth admits, "A few structure changes where made. But all and all, the songs were very strong." The producer describes the recording process as "smooth" saying all the band members were "cool" and everyone had their role which made the band the phenomenon it would become. Instantly he knew the band were all supreme musicians and approved of the fact that all noises and tones came from their amps and drums.

The album began with a slow building funk rock riff that is one of the more simple Rage tracks, but an incendiary opener, 'Bomb Track'. Throughout the album there are intricate lines here and there which indicate Rage's true political prowess. With 'Bombtrack' it was the tell tale line, "See through the news and the views that twist reality," referring to the manipulation of the media and the way propaganda leaks and ensnares the public.

The jewel in the crown of *Rage Against The Machine* came with one of the lead tracks, 'Killing In The Name'. This was the track which really broke the album on a worldwide scale, and rightly so. Here was an amalgamation of all the strengths of the band – opposing bass and guitar runs with a funk backbeat before a stirring riff leads the track into new realms.

With the simple verse and the repeated phrase, "and now you do what they told ya", the song built into a gargantuan chorus mixing lyrical bile and thunderous guitar to maximum effect. It was a song that didn't even necessitate printed lyrics, it was simply placed on the album with title alone. It was simple and oh-so-effective and would, of course, end with one of the most memorable one liners in musical history, Zack repeating, "Fuck you, I won't do what you tell me" slowly and purposefully rising to an enormous crescendo.

The song was a mantra of sorts, weaving its way through these repeated phrases which spoke for themselves. And the beauty of the parting line was it could refer to any person and any situation. A kid might hate his teacher, parents or is being bullied. An older person might hate their boss or the government. In extreme cases it could apply to someone suffering from abject poverty or an anarchistic uprising. The words felt good to say, it was an anti-authoritarian sentiment and it sounded majestic. Zack De La Rocha had adapted the likes of Body Count's "Tell us what to do, fuck you" and, with his impassioned fury, created a new catchphrase for the alternative nation of the Nineties.

It was almost very different however. As part of the label, RATM's A&R representative Michael Goldstone, "called every day to bug us," according to GGGarth. "His heart was in the right place. He did ask us to take out the 'Fuck you I won't do what you tell me,' part. This did not last long. We all told him he was wrong. He backed down!"

The power of the song was not lost on the band members playing it. For Tim Commerford, it is one of the greatest songs of all-time. "It's powerful," he remarked in *Kerrang!*. "Ask me what's my favourite song of any band and I'll tell you it's that. I love it. Obviously, I get a different perspective of it, but I know people want to hear it. When we play that song live, you see how kids react to it. It says a lot about this generation, you know? It's real nice. I know it's an important part of why we've had success. That set us out on the right foot. It was the foundation for the school we've been building since then."

Tom Morello animatedly recalled to Ben Myers, "I remember when our A&R guy suggested that this be our first single and

I was, like, 'Are you kidding?' To the band's credit we were always fearless in our business decisions and to choose the most profanity-laced song as the debut salvo – possibly the most profane single there has been – was something we were very proud of and gave a great indication of the direction we were headed. To this day I don't think there's a Rage song that really resonates in the way this does. The core of all rebellion is the denying of repressive authority and I think that is summed up very succinctly in [the closing line]."

'Take The Power Back' took a new direction on the album, one of many curveballs the listener would encounter, and it saw Rage in their most upbeat state of mind, with an almost polite guitar lick backing the lyrics. It also featured one of their most prominent funk workouts, with a bass sound almost reminiscent of the Red Hot Chili Peppers' Flea. But it was typical of RATM to change tack when least expected and the song denigrated into a dark, angry rant. Again Zack was referencing the lack of true political history taught to children in school, something with which Tom Morello would undoubtedly concur. Here was a satirical swipe outlining and criticising the fact that teachers merely have to play by the rules just as their students do, they must learn the right things and the right way to 'teach' and it has to conform to the system's requirements.

This sentiment was taken further in the driving 'Know Your Enemy', a truly subversive piece of rock 'n' roll literature. Each delivered word spoke volumes and if you didn't quite follow the path you could easily delve deeper. For those who instantly understood the veiled references that De La Rocha made to the establishment, it was all the more gratifying to hear them slayed on a mainstream, widely distributed record.

Musically the riff of the album makes an appearance on this track. The lead groove riff is a behemoth that will either make you dance or fight, such is its power. Then it breaks down with an impassioned run up the neck with another grooving lick. This catchy backing track was superbly led by the oration of De La Rocha, making the track one of the standout cuts. Even better, it features Tool's Maynard James Keenan in the breakdown section.

By now listeners were used to the genius of the Morello six

string technique and the surprise element was gone. But clearly, it wasn't as easy as it looked. Morello would say in *Guitar One* that "if I had not practiced for hours on technique, I wouldn't be able to play the solo on 'Know Your Enemy'. Even though that solo incorporates some very non-traditional elements, and sounds like almost a sequenced thing, my fingers are able to move fast enough to make it happen. Not in any kind of traditional rock-soloing way. All of that has really been stripped away."

And there was a revelation as far as the backbeat went, as Tom Morello revealed to Ben Myers: "I wrote the riffs for this song when Lock Up broke up, so it pre-dates me meeting the other Rage fellas. The interesting thing about 'Know Your Enemy' is that I had played it with a lot of other drummers – including some drummers in famous rock 'n' roll bands – and it never sounded particularly good until I played it with Brad Wilk, Tim Commerford and Zach De La Rocha, at which point it became this snarling, hard rock, punk-tinged rap fury that made it one of my favourite songs to play live. At Reading 1993 it made us truly realise for the first time that crowds would indeed jump up and down for Rage Against The Machine."

It wasn't all political satire at play; there were nods to Zack's personal demons as well. There was the brooding, building 'Settle For Nothing' which showed their appreciation of atmosphere. GGGarth describes the song as the "best" because "that song was completely live off the floor. Vocal and everything in one take. What a treat to sit and watch this happen."

On it Zack illuminated the hurt of his relationship with his father and penned the line "read my writing on the wall" which was a dual reference to both the graffiti of gangland culture and the Los Four murals his father used to paint. There was a cross reference point as well, in which he attempted to heal some of their relationship.

"It was really amazing," he told *Raygun*, "because I think that when my father kind of saw that the direction I was taking with Rage was converging with a lot of the things that he was involved in the Seventies, it brought him out of his seclusion a little bit. He actually started painting and writing again. I didn't expect him to be able to find his way through that. But the music and what I was doing with it reaffirmed the things that he once held important. That to me was just amazing. It fulfilled a void in me that had existed for a long time."

Zack would also later say, "When we started the band we were still confused, we had a lot of worries, one of which was to live out the political words. It stayed at a very personal level but, as I grew up and developed, I realised that personal conflicts are directly related to the society's conflicts." This was clearly reflected in his later lyrics especially.

After 'Killing In The Name', the most recognisable and well known song on *Rage Against The Machine* would be 'Bullet In The Head'. It seemed non-intrusive initially, focusing on a foreboding discordant bass line and the police siren style yelps of Morello's guitar, but it was another carefully constructed conversion from rap to rock, almost innocently creeping up on the listener before bursting into a relentless final stretch. Undoubtedly De La Rocha was the star of this particular crescendo, ripping the vocal as the veins in his head almost popped out of the speakers. Though the band would often say this version – from the original demo – could never be replicated so they didn't even try to re-record it, they seemed to do a fine job of re-energising it in most live shows since.

"We ended up using one of the demos with 'Bullet In The Head'," confirms GGGarth. "The version that we did just did not have the same power. A lot of demos turn out like that. I think the album as a whole turned out great, much better then the demos." The version of 'Bullet In The Head' which appears on the *Rage Against The Machine* DVD (from MTV Europe) is one of the greatest performances of the song ever witnessed and perhaps just beats the original.

"Lyrically, this was in response to the first Gulf war and the savvy propaganda of the initial Bush regime – the way they pulled the wool over people's eyes about such an imperialist endeavour," Tom Morello told Ben Myers, in his first post-Rage interview years later. "Because we refused to censor the lyrical content of our songs, we had difficulty getting videos broadcast so when we got to the UK we played a version of it on [BBC2 programme] *The Late Show* and some clever bloke at Sony UK took the performance and got it on MTV. Next thing you know, all of England was wearing the 'FUCT' T-shirt that Zack had on …"

The debut album from Rage Against The Machine ends with the riotous 'Freedom', a somewhat disheartening end to all the upbeat tension which has come before it. GGGarth recalls: "When Zack goes into the tag and starts screaming 'Freedom, yeah right,' the hairs went straight up in the air. Sure power."

Some would later say that the follow up RATM album was dark, but there were plenty of hints towards that direction even on the debut as exemplified by this song. "On 'Freedom' you hear drums being trashed," GGGarth explains. "Brad showed up with his first drum kit that he owned and we had the room mics up and he trashed his kit. Tim came up to me and said he was going to throw his bass through the control room window and how cool that would be? After I told him that would cost him around $5,000 to fix he changed his mind!"

Sometimes producers have to direct the band to a great extent, especially when that band is working on their first album together. Though Morello had some experience in performing for a major label, it was his first time with a well known producer and so you may think he was more likely to be moulded into the 'right way' of working but, according to GGGarth, the band were adamant about the direction they wanted to go.

"The band did have a very clear idea of what they wanted," he says. "I just tried to capture them as a band. Zack's voice went fast so we had to overdub some of the vocals. I made him come into the control room; I sat off to the side of the room running the tape machine. Zack used a Shure 58 [microphone] and I turned up the mains in the room as loud as they could go and he sang his ass off. We did not go line by line, but part by part."

He continues, "As for how much I had to adjust the sound, Tom did not want us to put any EQ on his tracks. That was a long talk about how it would sound better if we could use EQ. I spent a lot of time bouncing Tom's tracks so that when Andy [Wallace] mixed the record, he could throw up the track and every part was where it was going to be in the stereo mix."

Perhaps one of the greatest gifts of the debut is the fact it sounds so upfront and immediate. Sure the material would sound this way regardless of the mix but bands can easily lose their power if not in the hands of the right guy. It needs someone who isn't going to dilute the group's power by recording them too disparately or too many times. Especially with a band like Rage Against The Machine. What you really have to do with a band like that is plug in and let them play.

"I went out of my way to make this as much as a live recording and not a studio recording," GGGarth says in agreement. "We got a lot of their friends to come into the studio and sit in the live room and watch them record. I think we got three songs that way. Every song was hard; we only had thirty days to record the whole record. I think I was doing eighteen-hour days for thirty days."

Ultimately the union of producer and band yielded a lasting friendship and a mutual admiration and respect. "I am proud and lucky to have been in the same room as them," GGGarth says today. "The record I made with them was when they were a unit."

Despite their convictions and the seriousness of making a revolutionary first album, Rage could also switch off and have fun just as they do today. "We had lots of fun in the studio," GGGarth remembers. "The first day Zack shaved my head. One day Tim went and got me food and when I opened the bag, he had taken a shit in it. I got him back though. They were playing an outdoor show in the heat of the summer, I took my dog for a walk in the morning and picked up his morning movement and put it in Tim's bass case. It sat in the heat all day and when he opened it up he got mad but then had a good laugh. I always win!"

The release of *Rage Against The Machine* would prompt immediate attention towards their singer's lyrics. Zack felt his words spoke for themselves. "To me, you allow people to interpret for themselves," he would say in an interview with a Mexican newspaper. "I do not enjoy being a public personality. It's not something I feel is conducive to accomplishing what we want to accomplish. In fact, I think that philosophically the idea of public personality is ridiculous. The daily enquiries into my personal life, and to other artists' personal lives, becomes tabloid. And what then becomes missing from that is the hope that music can still effect change. So I think that whatever happens to the ideas of a band, if they are to engage directly in political struggles and correcting injustice it's important to realise that public personality has nothing to do with it."

There are few more powerful things you can do to make a statement with your art than to package it with a striking image and the cover of the RATM debut featured an indelible, iconic photograph. On June 11, 1963 on a busy Saigon street, the Vietnamese Buddhist monk Thich Quang Duc burned himself to death in protest at the treatment of Buddhists by the administration in power in South Vietnam. Duc sat calmly in the Buddhist lotus position while a colleague poured five gallons of gasoline on and around him and promptly set fire to the 66-year-old.

Even in the grip of death, Thich Quang Duc was respectful, polite and moving. His last words written shortly before his death simply stated, "Before closing my eyes and moving towards the vision of the Buddha, I respectfully plead to President Ngo Dinh Diem to take a mind of compassion towards the people of the nation and implement religious equality to maintain the strength of the homeland eternally. I call the venerables, reverends, members of the sangha and the lay Buddhists to organise in solidarity to make sacrifices to protect Buddhism."

This was a distinctly honourable protest and one of immense courage and faith. Duc's protest yielded some positive change though not as profound as he may have hoped. Despite the lack of serious transformation, the impact of the photograph reverberated around the world. It was something many could respect, that someone could have such deep faith and beliefs he could self-sacrifice his life in protest. In today's world, this is no longer a rarity with the suicide bomber ethos in the heart of many groups, yet in the Sixties it inspired global outrage. Even then US president John F. Kennedy was alleged to have said "Jesus Christ!" when he heard the news and would later say, "No news picture in history has generated so much emotion around the world as that one."

Coincidentally, just five months after Thich Quang Duc's death, JFK would be assassinated. It's unlikely many of the people picking up the *Rage Against The Machine* album knew the true meaning behind the photo, but it was powerful, whatever your understanding.

On November 6, 1992, the debut album *Rage Against The Machine* hit the stores and promptly began a public interest which would gradually build and build. It wasn't initially a huge player at the top of the charts but sales were consistent. Those who knew about it really wanted it, thanks to the promotional use of the likes of 'Killing In The Name' and 'Bullet In The Head'. It was an album Epic seemed to believe in yet, cleverly, they didn't over-promote it. "At the end of the record we felt we had made something special here," GGGarth remembers, with some understatement.

The album stayed in the *Billboard* Top 200 for 89 weeks, climbing to Number 45 at one stage. *Billboard* even acknowledged RATM as "one of the most original and virtuosi new rock bands in the nation." Awarding the album top marks, *Kerrang!* gushed, "This is it, the true birth of rap-metal and nu-metal. A pan-international, multi-ethnic riot of pumping bass, utterly unique guitar sounds and spray paint-able slogans to unite the tribes and incite a revolt."

Yet Rage would not entirely grant the media what they wanted, starting with the fact that their singer would not even agree to be interviewed for the first few years of the band's career. "It was to ensure the protection of this band's integrity," he told *Kerrang!* in 1999. "Our words had to first be backed up by actions because we're dealing with a monstrous pop culture that sucks in anything culturally resistant in order to commodify and pacify it and make it non-threatening. It felt like we needed to raise the volume for those whose voices aren't heard. There was a time when we became popular that I think we probably could have sold two or three times as many records than we did but I think it would have been very destructive for the band, I really do."

Ultimately the reason for the success of the debut album was not the stirring political statements, the mixed ethnicity of the band or even the incendiary front cover art. The reason Rage Against The Machine went on to sell millions of copies was that the music was incisive and out of this world. "A good song should make you wanna tap your foot and get with your girl," Tom Morello said. "A great song should destroy cops and set fire to the suburbs. I'm only interested in writing great songs."

There were ten great songs on *Rage Against The Machine* and

Morello had a theory as to why it worked for them and not other bands of the same vein. "There are many overtly political bands that do not sell millions of records like Rage Against the Machine because the first thing they have to take care of is the musical chemistry," he suggested. "You can have all of your politics lined up and all of your analyses together, but it's got to be a great rock and roll band."

Chapter Eight
Rebels With Due Cause

Tim Commerford would state that when Rage Against The Machine formed their "goals were pretty modest. We were going to write and play music that was absolutely uncompromised (sic) in any way. It was music that was combining the hardest and most radical fringes of hip-hop and hard rock and it was mixed into this revolutionary political cocktail. I honestly didn't think we'd be able to book a show, considering the band's ethnic make-up and the heaviness of the music."

Given the scene Rage entered, this was not surprising, but the entire band were pleasantly surprised by the reaction they received. It began with Europe, specifically the UK. Rage played their first show in Great Britain in 1992 when they supported Suicidal Tendencies. A few months later they would return to headline their own show at the Camden Underworld. When they then played Glasgow, the show became memorable for a relatively unusual reason. "Weirdly, for a very brief period of a few weeks we even had a teeny-bopper following!" Tom Morello recalled. "I remember them camped outside our hotels and getting chased down the street by young girls in Glasgow."

RATM followed Suicidal Tendencies around Europe and some acrimony must have occurred because from being label mates and seemingly perfect touring partners, just a year later ST's Mike Muir would admonish and mock Rage Against The Machine in a song with his side project Infectious Grooves, more of which further on in the chapter.

The likes of *Kerrang!* were bowled over, insisting Rage had better execution to the idea of rap rock than Body Count. There was instantaneous interest amongst rock fans for this exciting new hybrid of styles and the playing of the 'Killing In The Name' video on the predominantly metal TV show *Raw Power* did no harm to RATM's ability to crossover. The mainstream BBC channel Radio 1 also played the song, however they forgot to edit the word 'fuck' ("and a 'motherfucker' for good measure" Tom Morello later laughed) and the song was left untouched. It was the only time a pop radio station let so many fucks slip by in one session.

There were inevitably questions regarding the edit which most people would hear however – those being that if the band had a message should it not be left untouched? As usual Tom Morello had a strong riposte. "I think it's an important part of the screening process for artists," he would say, typically thinking of the wider picture. "You have to be obedient in many different ways in order to get your music played on the radio, in order to get your videos played on TV. And one of those ways is the language. You know bands that tend to unapologetically use strong language are excluded from the mainstream. Often, or occasionally, those bands have a subversive political message as well, which is then also excluded from the mainstream. I think that the language is very important."

Rage returned to the US and took up with Irish American hip-hop troupe House Of Pain in March of 1993 before joining the Lollapalooza (a word meaning "remarkable or wonderful person or thing") tour, a travelling festival which took a large line-up and visited various cities throughout the US. It was created by Jane's Addiction's Perry Farrell, an old friend of Tom Morello. Ironically, in 1993 RATM's buddies Tool topped the Lollapalooza bill.

Though the initial idea was cool enough, with spaces and booths for non-profit political groups and craft stalls, it soon hit upon a huge problem – it became very successful and was thus infected by corporate greed. One area this was most prominent was in the merchandise stalls. As part of their considerate ethics, Rage Against The Machine set their own, reasonable prices for their merchandise, selling short sleeve shirts for $10 and long sleeves for $13.

"The Lollapalooza people said no to that," Tom explained, "because the Lollapalooza shirts were going for $23, and they were afraid that choosing between that and a Rage shirt would hurt their sales. So we decided not to sell any T-shirts at all, and Zack told every audience where most of the money for the Lollapalooza shirts was going, to the promoters and the landowners of the venues. Their sales declined dramatically throughout the tour!"

But this was just a small part of Rage's battle against the system and the '93 Lollapalooza tour will forever be remembered for one incident in particular. On 18 July, appearing on stage in Philadelphia, Rage didn't walk out with instruments and microphones; they went out naked, save for some duct tape.

In protest at the PMRC, the band left guitars in the background but turned them on to emit grating feedback as they stood on stage in a line, each member spelling out, one letter each on his chest: P-M-R-C. They kept their mouths closed with duct tape and stood still for 15 minutes. The reaction was initially one of anger, but as Tom would say, that was the point. And in order to placate their fans, Rage played a free headline show in Philadelphia. "It was our way of letting the audience know that if they didn't take the issue of censorship into their own hands, they would not be able to hear artists like us," Morello said of the dissent.

And he elaborated to Ben Myers, "We had thought about doing it a few days before, but we decided to wait in order to pick the right city in which to stage our protest – in this case Philadelphia, home of the Liberty Bell and all of that. It seemed appropriate. As there is now in the wake of the Columbine shooting, back then there was a high level of censorship in the arts and entertainment in the US. At that time the 2 Live Crew were being censored and we decided we should do something as high level as Lollapalooza '93 to ... well, basically it was Situationist shit-stirring to cause a bit of buzz. We stood on stage for fifteen minutes and let me tell you, fifteen minutes is an eternity when you're standing butt-naked in front of thirty thousand people. That is a long-ass time! Because we were opening the whole show, for the first five minutes people were going crazy. Then, five minutes in people were, like, 'OK, where's 'Bullet In The Head' then?' We're looking at them; they're looking at us ... for another five minutes. Then they start getting pissed and the boo-ing begins, the middle fingers are raised and they start throwing coins, which was terrifying. The majority of the crowd were really angry, pissed off and upset, but that was our exact point: you may not be able to hear controversial music on mainstream radio or TV, but you don't just sit there waiting for it. You have to act if you want to hear it, which is what we prompted them to do. We walked offstage and, of course, the police came to arrest us and put it this way, Rage Against The Machine's biggest fans are not members of the Philadelphia Police Department! Luckily I got out because I was able to hide out on Fishbone's tour bus ..."

Morello would elucidate further on his views of the PMRC, telling one magazine, "Normally, the kinds of music that are always attacked are black music, hip-hop, hard rock, and, like, working-class white music, like heavy metal or whatever. Because those things, I think not coincidentally, speak to the American underclass. And some, obviously your Metallica songs, don't have an anti-sweatshop message. Still, there's something in the form that they find threatening, maybe the way in which young people express their independence. They don't like extreme music and they want to shut that down. And they want you to be obedient and they want you to not veer from the mainstream."

It was also reassuring to note some of the things going through the band members' heads while they were standing, privates blowing in the wind. Things many red-blooded males would contemplate given such a predicament. "I was thinking about how the wind felt underneath my scrotum, what the people in the front were thinking, and all the cameras flashing and what they were going to be thinking as they developed their film," Brad Wilk laughed. It was a rare moment of fun for the drummer, despite the seriousness of the point made by RATM. For the Lollapalooza tour Wilk had to deal with a number of traumas: three days before it began his father was killed; while the band were halfway through the tour, a friend of Wilk's committed suicide; and then there was a third death, when a band friend was tragically murdered.

Tim Commerford felt the need to assert his manhood, promising all the girls in attendance that "it's bigger than that ... the size of my penis, that's what was going through my mind in Philadelphia." It was a stand of which Mary Morello was no doubt proud, and she would later endorse her boys directly when she

Rage Against The Machine at an early press shoot, London, 1992.
Sony Music Archive / Getty Images / Mark Baker

Zack at the Shoreline Amphitheatre as part of Lollapalooza, 1993.
Photo by Tim Mosenfelder / Getty Images

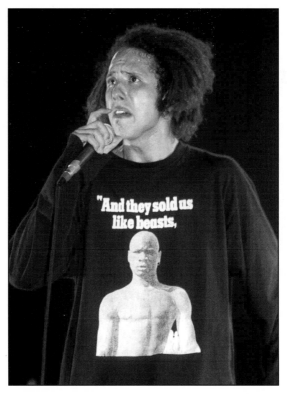

Zack and Rage at the Brixton Academy, 1993.
Brian Rasic/Rex Features

Tim Commerford, Tom Morello, Zack De La Rocha and Brad Wilk, 1996.
Niels Van Iperen/Retna

Rage perform at the Tibetan Freedom Concert at the Polo Fields
in Golden Gate Park, San Francisco, June, 1996.
Tim Mosenfelder/Getty Images

Still giving it their all, 2000.
Jay Blakesberg/Retna

Tom Morello with fans and marchers during a protest
outside the Taco Bell headquarters, 2004.
Kelly A. Swift/Retna

Brad behind the kit at an Audioslave show in Mexico City, May, 2005.
Fernando Aceves/Retna

Audioslave salute the crowd during the KROQ Weenie Roast, 2005.
Kelly A. Swift/Retna

Tim live at the Vegoose Music Festival, Las Vegas, October, 2007.
RNY/Jeff Kroll/Retna

Tom Morello, 'The Nightwatchman', signs autographs for his fans while promoting
his new album, *One Man Revolution*, April, 2007.
RNY/Jackie Butler/Retna

Rage back to business, performing at Coachella Festival, California, April, 2007.
Kelly A. Swift/Retna

Zack De La Rocha at the 2007 Rock The Bells Festival, NY, July, 2007.
Wes Worskoski/Retna

Zack and Tom at the C.I.W. rally in The House of Blues, Chicago, April, 2007.
RNY/Gene Ambo/Retna

Tom, Wayne Kramer of MC5, Sen Dog of Cypress Hill & Perry Farrell
at the opening of the newest John Varvatos boutique, located on the space that
was once CBGB & OMFUG, NYC, April, 2008.
Randy Haecker/Retna

gave a short speech before they came onstage. Tom Morello said of his mother, "She looks very much the part of the retired suburban high school teacher [but] will get on the stage with a militant fist raised high and say, 'Please welcome the best fucking band in the universe!'"

Despite their best intentions and stand against the system, Rage were beginning to receive harsh criticism from various quarters regarding their authenticity. Chief among the detractors condemnations was the fact RATM were signed to a major label despite all their anti-corporate posturing. It is a debate, which will always, um, rage, and there are reasons for agreeing with either side.

Award ceremonies, which Rage have often been a part of, can be seen as confirmation of how far you are entrenched within the system – to some at least.

GGGarth Richardson was in the right place to comment on their ascent from basic debut record musicians to Grammy award winning artistes and it didn't sit well.

"Being on a big label was OK because they needed the machine to break the record," he considers. "However I did find it hard to see them go up and take their first Grammy [in 1997]. I think the Grammys are everything the band does not stand for. I feel Zack had those feelings. After the first Grammy ... everything they stood for went out the window."

One of the worst criticisms was that some record labels, or rather the corporations that they are sub-divisions within, are strongly rumoured to have direct connections to the arms industry. Zack De La Rocha has retorted strongly to this, such as in the pages of the excellent *Propaganda* magazine, where he said, "I guarantee that there are a lot of companies that make a lot of shit, including stuff for the weapons industry ... it became clear in the Sixties that armed fighting had failed, at least temporarily. So what is the most important information tool in our time? That's information. To me, not using Sony or abusing them to tell people what's going on in the US and Europe, would be the same if the Zapatistas didn't use the guns they've stolen from the Mexican army."

It would seem puzzling to some that a band who purported to

oppose the system and all its foul play should be at the top of that labels' musical hierarchy. Who is this really benefiting? Well, certainly it benefits RATM financially and gives them maximum exposure. It doesn't benefit the fans other than to know that the RATM products will be readily available and the band will receive enough financial support that they will always be able to tour and produce records – as long as they keep selling, of course.

For the fans, the cost of a RATM CD or DVD is set by the record company or the manufacturers/distributors, it is not down to the band and that is chiefly because it is the label's responsibility to make their own money. Rage do not control every part of their operation, in fact they control relatively little. As referenced several times elsewhere in this book and as Tom Morello is often at pains to point out, the band has complete *artistic* and *creative* control. From the average artist's point of view, you couldn't really ask for more, but we are not talking about a band that relies solely on their 'art' to speak for them.

Many have criticised the band for not taking a stand in the way that hardcore legends Fugazi manage their operation. That band is signed to Dischord records, the label owned by Minor Threat/Fugazi leader Ian Mackaye, who has always made sure that all Dischord material is cheap enough for people to afford – CDs are around $9-$10 and the label makes sure that their catalogue is always available at that price, even in high street retailers. So the fact is, in certain circumstances it can be done. The system can be traversed from within, albeit on a much lower level commercially.

For RATM's first album, they were surely excited to be on a major label and therefore many people could forgive them for releasing the debut in this fashion. But once they became popular across the world the argument is simply, why did the band not remove themselves from the major grasp and 'do a Fugazi'?

As Morello has often said, it is incredibly hard work to essentially sell records out the back of the van. He has a point. Not only are the logistics of running an independent organisation immensely time consuming and difficult to administer, Rage have all that they want already in place so in many ways, what would have been the point in downsizing their empire as soon as they had built it? "I don't care what people at indie-record stores necessarily think," Morello has said. "What we're trying to do is get Leonard Peltier out of jail. How do we do that? Do you want fewer people organising to get him out? Or do you want more?"

He said of Fugazi, "I like the band, and I respect their integrity and their being stalwarts, but the thing that they do, which we are totally incapable of doing, is that they're businessmen; they run a label; we do not have the capabilities or the desire to do that. I want to play great music and [piss] off 'The Man', and I have no time to deal with receipts from Bulgarian record sales."

In many ways it would have been easier for Rage Against The Machine to ignore these kinds of enquiries and give the "my art speaks for itself" line. But Morello would often go into long diatribes about his beliefs and he is always refreshingly straight down the line and honest. How many political activists admit they don't have time to do things a certain way, using a method which would be far more respected and even possibly expected by their peers? Ultimately no one could criticise Fugazi for their ethics but there were thousands around the world who conveniently criticised RATM.

Morello makes a supreme point about the difference between RATM and Fugazi when he says in *Rolling Stone* that, "I love and respect Fugazi, but I don't know that they've done more than Rage Against The Machine. They have business acumen as label owners, but I don't know that they've accomplished more." Looking at that line of scrutiny you would have to either concede Morello is correct or at least admit that the two bands operate on different levels of activism.

Tom Morello also has said many times, when addressing the fact RATM are on a major, "A better question might be to all other bands on major labels, 'Why aren't you doing something with the tremendous amount of exposure you have to effect some sort of change?' Rather than just attacking a band that is using it for some sort of political goals. Why not look at all the bands that aren't doing that?"

As mentioned, Suicidal Tendencies took RATM out on a European venture when they first sprang on the scene but somewhere along the line ST front man Mike Muir developed a great disdain for the band. His side project Infectious Grooves wrote a song called 'Do What I Tell Ya' and proceeded to criticise the RATM missive. The main criticism was featured in the following: "Now you're making your political statement/Or are you trying to add to your financial statement/And let's not forget the evil corporations/Then why is Sony the sponsor of your presentation?"

In one interview, Muir would say in connection with the song, "Don't try and make a political statement just because you're in a band. Run for office, change the world if you think you can."

Such criticism was widespread amongst the group's detractors. Many simplistically saw Rage on a major and jumped on the bandwagon without realising what the band had been through and that they had more reasons than most to do what they do, and more effectively than almost any other comparative band you could name. What modern band really has managed to combine a successful, widespread music career with positive political statements and/or change?

It also raises a strange question regarding criticism of artists from within the music industry. In no other profession are the voices relaying a message so vilified as within the music industry. For some inexplicable reason, it is unacceptable to play in a band and have political lyrics whilst occupying space on a major label roster, yet perfectly acceptable for instance to be a mainstream actor or actress and perform a role which gives out a positive message.

Yet musicians are not allowed the privilege of doing anything other than constantly playing their role within the industry and they must be 'on it' at all times. This is clearly unfair pressure for which artists and bands are not given their due. Everyone has the right to switch off from time to time and equally, most of us are made up of shades of grey rather than black or white. What is Rage Against The Machine if not the equivalent of an actor playing a role in a movie? Beyond this however, they participate in active causes and have attempted to stir change in hundreds of thousands of lives around the world. With all due respect to the acting profession, how many actors do this? Don't they merely move onto their next part?

"First of all, if you're going to criticise our tactics, you need to look in the mirror and see what it is that you're doing in your life that is being more productive from an activist point of view than Rage Against The Machine," Morello pointed out. "If you are able to do that, then I'm willing to listen, but if it's just some college kid whose mommy and daddy are paying for their school who's got a Fugazi poster on the wall, and they've got problems with us, then forget it."

Indeed, Morello was referring to the multitude of criticisms on the internet of the RATM manifesto. These were overwhelmingly from privileged suburban white kids who decided it was more productive to sit and criticise Rage Against The Machine than to go out into society and try to effect some kind of change themselves. Such is the dichotomy and mentality of many of those who tend to criticise the band. Again in defence of his band's position on a major, Morello has said, "That question has never once come to the band from anyone who is involved in political activism. That only comes from smug rock journalists and from, for the most part, your middle-class people who may have some sort of indie rock élitist credentials, but beyond that have done jack shit in the world of political activism. First of all, there's very little precedent for what we're doing. There's not a map for revolutionary rock bands on major labels who sell nine million records. There's no precedent for it, so we're figuring out elements of it on our own."

In many ways, Rage are an easy target. It's an immediate response to question a band on a major label who talk so critically of the corporate way of life and there is nothing wrong with questioning and looking into the issue to see whether the band is hypocritical or counterfeit or indeed the opposite. But overwhelmingly, it is clear that those who speak out loudest on the subject have done the least research.

Nobody bats an eyelid that authors such as Noam Chomsky have their works available in major book stores, and it's not as if his books are free. It is the prerogative of the anarchist to assault the system in any way possible. Much better to speak out against the injustices of particular regimes and capitalistic crimes and to be doing so through the medium of a corporation. There are few instances in society where this would be allowed. If you speak out within an office at your boss or the higher echelons of your particular company, you would receive a few warnings and eventually be dismissed if you persisted, but, because society itself is based on capitalism, as long as you are making money for the powers that be, they often couldn't care less what you're talking about. This leaves Rage Against The Machine untouched and they can say what they want, which of course they do. Ultimately it's not a question of integrity, it's a question of availability.

"Leonard Peltier doesn't care what label we're on," says Morello convincingly. "We've been able to introduce his case to an entirely new generation of young people, which increases the pressure, through letter-writing and emails and what have you, on President Clinton to try to get an order of clemency. The Anti-Nazi League in Europe doesn't care what label we're on, because when it comes time to hold a benefit show, we draw enough people to help put bodies in the streets the next day to throw bricks at fascists. They don't care. At all. It's tactical as much as anything else. You have two choices when you're a band with political ideals: you either put your head in the sand and you sell 45s out of the back of a truck and you're very proud of yourself for how pure you are, or you engage the world and you do your best to make strategies to effect real change."

Amongst others, Rage have been criticised for their support of the Peruvian Shining Path guerrillas and their imprisoned leader Abimael Guzman, as expressed in the video for 'Bombtrack'. Shining Path is an armed communist organisation but they effectively represent the Communist Party. The government of Peru consider them a terrorist organisation and SP are reputedly responsible for attacks on civilians and peasants as well as trade union organisers and elected officials.

There are no known interviews where Tom Morello responds to this, however Zack De La Rocha was questioned by *Propaganda* magazine on the subject. "I don't personally support them. I support some of the things they fight for," he said of Shining Path. "I think they should wrestle themselves out of the US's clutches and get control over their own faith, like all the other countries in Central and South America. But I think that Shining Path repeat a lot of errors that they should have learned from throughout history. I think that if Shining Path got control, it wouldn't change anything about the Peruvian people's situation. It would just be someone else in power."

De La Rocha would also talk to *Propaganda* about various forms of uprising within society, and said the following regarding an armed stand. "I would support an armed rebellion, if the message gets properly through. An armed rebellion for a society where people don't have to sell themselves to prostitution, cheap workforce etc to survive. A society that changes the differences between men and women, an armed rebellion that learns from the Soviet communists' errors, that forced a system down on people. But I won't join any armed group if I don't feel the conditions are right. The most important thing right now is to educate, inform and make people aware until time is ready for an armed fight ... and Rage is part of that process."

Chapter Nine
Your Anger Is A Gift

In 1993, the impact of Rage Against The Machine's awesome debut album was felt in the form of a soundtrack album which showcased the scene both Rage and Body Count were virtually responsible for. *Judgement Night* was an underrated film but its qualities were overshadowed by the all-star line-up which created the soundtrack. The idea was to meld various rock and metal bands with hip-hop stars of the day in duets. Some of the most memorable tracks were Faith No More and Boo-Yaa T.R.I.B.E's 'Another Body Murdered', Helmet and House Of Pain's 'Just Another Victim' and the album title track, performed by Biohazard and Onyx. It showed the peaks to which rap metal could aim, and just how fast and heavy it could get without losing the spirit of either genre. This album was ultimately a one-off. There would be other collaborations here and there and other compilation albums which aimed for a similar theme but none were as strong as *Judgement Night* which ultimately featured 11 great songs.

There is also a link with Rage Against The Machine and the *Judgement Night* soundtrack. The band hooked up with Tool to record a song called 'Can't Kill The Revolution', though sadly this was never used for the album. The track is obscure to say the least and hard to find. One listen however shows why the song was not used on the album. Firstly the production is horrendous, sounding like a jam in a garage taped onto a C60 cassette tape! The combination of whispered verse and shouted chorus sounds amateurish – more like a fledgling band who are trying to ape both Tool and RATM rather than the professionals. The potential of the song is evident but it is a very poor representation of both bands as it stands. Some die hard fans of the two groups have pondered as to whether the song was ever actually played by both bands together as it sounds so erratic that the presumption is the two groups played their parts separately and then handed a studio wizard the task of splicing them together! Yet, though it would be easy to assume this, it sounds far more likely that the song came from a jam session between Maynard James Keenan, Adam Jones and the members of RATM. If this is the case, it is a rather disappointing attempt to boost the *Judgement Night* soundtrack.

As a separate unit, Rage were continuing unabated, ripping up stages across the US and Europe. At the Pink Pop festival in Holland, the band caused such a furore in the crowd during their set that the resultant force was enough to register on the Richter scale at 1.1. The festival was nothing at all to speak of until Rage launched into their set at which point the graphs went mad. It was demonstrative of RATM's standing on European shores, but it would be some time until they felt the same impact across their homeland.

"It was almost surreal, because at that time, when we played that concert, I don't think we had sold 50,000 records in the United States," Morello would expand. "So there were more people jumping up and down on a field in Holland during 'Killing In The Name' than even knew about the band in the United States. We were living the cliché. 'We're bigger in Europe! We're huge in Holland!'" It wasn't just the crowd who went crazy during the band's set. Though the least mobile of the group, drummer Brad Wilk still managed to painfully pull his back. "At the end of 'Bullet In Your Head' I ripped the muscles of the right side of my back all the way around my chest," he recalled. "We had to stop the tour for, like, two weeks."

Naturally, after such a successful debut, fans started to demand new material and it had to be good to keep the momentum were building. The band reconvened after over a year of touring and more press coverage than they could have ever hoped for. Now they truly had a platform upon which to speak of issues they were most passionate about. But there were tensions within the group and it was something unexpected which none of the four quite knew how to handle.

"Making [second album] *Evil Empire* was very, very difficult,"

Tom Morello later recalled to Ben Myers. "A lot of arguments. Our success put us under a microscope and we all handled it very differently. My take was to push the boundaries of rock 'n' roll and go further, politically and musically, than any other band had before. Others wanted to retreat and considered our 'success' was an innately evil thing and we needed to pull back to our independent roots.

"A lot of tensions emanated from the conceptions that each of us developed after the first album about what a great record would sound like," De La Rocha would add. "Having not continuously written due to our political engagements, we came back with different ideas."

Where he was given full and free reign over the course of the debut album, De La Rocha felt he was inhibited in rehearsals for the follow-up. Ultimately he sought recognition from his band mates and he felt it was not forthcoming, leading to a simmering resentment which started to affect the material, the atmosphere and those around the band. Quickly, rumours emerged which suggested a split may have occurred. One outlandish gossip missive stated that certain music industry executives had flown to Chiapas, southern Mexico, where De La Rocha was staying, and offered him a full suitcase of money to come back to the band. If true, one can hardly think of a more inappropriate gesture of reconciliation to someone like De La Rocha. Such stories were unfounded but it would take some effort to appease both Morello and De La Rocha. The former would make light of the strains which seemed to exist between himself and the singer, laughing, "It's not unique among rock bands to find the occasional dissension within the band. Yes, it is part of the story – sometimes it's a big part. But compared to the music we make and causes that we pursue, the personality of the band beyond that is not so interesting. Does anybody care if Dokken got along or not?"

He had good reason to be so calm about his band's status. Despite the rumoured wrangles within the group, they were writing some immense material. RATM were adamant they weren't about to repeat the formula for the debut. Yes, they were going to feature the smart rapping of De La Rocha and the experimental, driving glitches and rhythms of Morello, the drums and bass would still be focussed and bathed in hip–hop grooves, but there had to be some progression, some improvement. It was arguable whether the band could actually improve on such a landmark recording as the debut. Such a dilemma is a nice one to have: how do you improve on perfection?

The easiest way to respond was to steer in a similar direction but with a new focus and a different way of recording. The band decided to go with a new producer and settled on Brendan O'Brien. "I heard it was hell making that record," GGGarth says of O'Brien's job. "I would of loved to have done it but glad I did not. The label wanted to use someone other than me, I am fine with this. A lot of bands and labels do this. It is part of the biz. That record got me out of the gate, I have not looked back." The band is still friends with their old producer, as he explains. "Whenever I am in LA, I do run into them. We all hug and laugh about Tim shitting in a bag and giving it to me."

GGGarth is still a very well respected producer and he and (further legendary producer) Bob Ezrin are opening up a recording school in Vancouver, explaining that he is "getting tired of all of the schools teaching kids nothing and have to pay a ton of money. My father trained Bob Ezrin, my father and Bob Ezrin trained me. We are going to show the kids how to make it in the new music biz."

Though Brendan O'Brien had worked with varying kinds of music makers, come the mid-Nineties he was best known as a grunge producer, having overseen the likes of Pearl Jam's *Vitalogy* and Stone Temple Pilots' debut grunge classic *Core* and its follow up *Purple*. Morello and Co. felt O'Brien could capture their innate tension and their incendiary live performances. O'Brien was perhaps part of the reason the band managed to settle their reported differences so amicably, he imbibed the recording sessions with a real sense of fun and made light of the creative differences emerging. Instead the focus shifted and the band felt re-energised and more than able to promote their work.

Still, both Zack De La Rocha and his rhythm section were, at first, unconvinced themselves about the material and the overall feel of the record. "I remember going into making that record and hearing the sounds that were coming out and hating it, despising

107

it," De La Rocha said. "Being a great artist is a form of great frustration and I'm not sure I'll ever be completely satisfied. But that keeps me going, even though at the time we were considering calling it a day. The other thing that kept us going was the knowledge that we could raise awareness and address issues, and engage young people politically." Brad Wilk demonstrated his confusion over the record when he said, "Between the musical tracks and lyrics being finished and a few months later I've gone through hating the record to loving the record. This period is really hard to be objective with the music."

So why was the album – called *Evil Empire* – so difficult not only for fans, but even the band, to accept? Album number two was always going to be hard to establish without comparisons to the debut. And when it emerged that the material was harsher, darker and more involved, many fans were confused or even completely turned off. Ultimately though, the apparent inaccessibility of the material would be one of its greatest strengths.

Promotion of the album started with 'Bulls On Parade'. The song was a stand against the commonly known Military Industrial Complex which refers to industrialists and the military who manufacture arms and make profits by selling them to governments. The term was coined by then US president Dwight D. Eisenhower in 1961.

De La Rocha put in one of his best vocal performances in RATM history, spitting his words with effectiveness. There was also a dual word-play to certain phrases, such as the use of "terror rains" which equally referred to the US people being reigned over by terror. The beautiful irony of foreign "terrorists" being cited as the biggest threat to the US and indeed the world when right under the resident's noses arms were being mass produced and profiteered was one of the central themes of the song.

Musically, it was the most instant piece on the second album. The combination of the lyrics, which were almost out of step with the music, and the cascading and simple guitar refrains is utterly stunning, Zack's voice sounding at its most fresh and vibrant to date. As he enunciated on one particularly strong line, "While arms warehouses fill as quick as tha cells," there was a palpable sense of anger in his voice, and not from shouting or screaming the line, it's from the genuine outrage behind the song. The track was all the better for the almost casual delivery of the verses. It wouldn't be Rage without a riotous climax however and the immense, powerful riff causes an upsurge with Zack spilling the title line again and again. Here perhaps was the clue that this band meant what they said at the time of the first album. This was no casual deflection at a moot political cause, it was real, structured and uncensored.

There are many so-called political bands in existence but their rhetoric seems to be designed as much to give them an identity rather than any inherent desire for change. It is a way to quickly sell records. If young kids think they are being rebellious by buying 'dangerous' music then it will have the same effect whether it's W.A.S.P. singing about fucking like a beast or a modern punk band singing of political atrocities. This was the accusation levelled at Rage Against The Machine: one of leading the public on with the insinuation they felt strongly about these topics yet ultimately not giving a damn and just using it as an easy way to sell records instantaneously. Rebellion is an alluring concept to most adolescents, and indeed any potentially unruly adults.

The question was often levelled: were RATM sincere about their affections? One listen to 'People Of The Sun' should have been enough to silence any critics. Though the song featured a catchy riff which sounds as if it's plucked purposefully, it wasn't a plectrum or the wrist doing damage – rather an Allen wrench raked up and down the Morello A-string. Such was its simplicity (belying its immense stature), the song came together in less than an hour. Chiefly the lyrics were about the struggles of the Zapatista people in Mexico, highlighted artfully in De La Rocha's poetic, fact-strewn lyrics.

If there was a criticism regarding the band's message, it would be that such was the ferocity and intricacy of De La Rocha's delivery, that the lyrics were difficult to pinpoint upon first listen, especially without a lyric book. Additionally even with a lyric sheet it might be hard for some to correlate the sentiments expressed with the exact issue in question.

Which wasn't to say the lyrics should be more straightforward or obvious – after all it was part of the De La Rocha style to incorporate old school hip-hop ethics and word alterations and abbreviations along with his challenging themes. But if a person heard the songs on the radio, without any context or lyrical clues, they'd doubtless have little idea what the actual message was. Therefore there was possibly an element of preaching to the converted, or at least those who know enough to do their research and read further into the events mentioned.

The video to the song gave a clearer sense of the lyrical content, despite the origin being relatively obscure. The black and white documentary style footage is from director Sergei M. Eisenstein's 1979 film *Que Viva Mexico*, which offered an explanation and celebration of Mexican culture. There were also statistics related to the Zapatista Army Of National Liberation and some film of arms arriving from the US into Mexico. For the public, thanks to MTV censors, scenes of a Mexican worker being buried alive, then trampled and footage of dead teenagers in a morgue were replaced by varying military footage – seemingly incendiary but actually completely indistinct.

It was Viacom, the company who own MTV, that objected to the video and who sent the band a list with every single thing they wanted to change. "Not to sound like too much of a conspiracy theorist, I think they don't like the politics of the band and they look for excuses to not play the video," Tom Morello said. RATM later released their own home video showcasing the full, unedited version of this and other videos, which had previously been censored.

Over the preceding years approaching the release of *Evil Empire*, Zack De La Rocha had immersed himself in his ancestry and culture, travelling to Chiapas and indulging in the daily life of the indigenous peoples. He visited the village of La Garrucha, a place so relatively obscure that there is barely any information regarding its origin and peoples anywhere except within old Mexican history textbooks.

"There are certain things about playing music that are making me really comfortable," De La Rocha would later expand. "The root of our fear in the hardcore scene was always the question of how we could live and keep this lifestyle. That was the fundamental rally cry in our hearts, you know? 'We're not going to be wage slaves! We're not going to work nine-to-five!' But sometimes that comfort takes away so much of what made this music so vital and what made what we were doing so important. Going to Mexico and feeling like my life was in danger, it makes me feel that again. It makes me feel alive again, and I miss that."

There were few references to his involvement across the internet ,yet within De La Rocha's own community his activism was becoming more pronounced. At the beginning of 1996, when recording had been completed for *Evil Empire*, the singer assembled a group of young students, artists and activists from East Los Angeles in order to visit civil camps for peace in La Garrucha. De La Rocha was under no illusions as to what to expect but it's clear even he was shocked and appalled by what he observed. "I experienced the terror and the intimidation to the integrity of the people by the soldiers;" he told *Enlace Civil* in Chiapas, "the isolation in which the communities had to subsist; the military camps located between the houses and the fields, I understood then that one of the great missions of a low intensity war is to wear out the people through hunger and to create lack of goods. That starvation practice against the people has the same effect as throwing bombs on the population.

"We saw how militarization (sic) had increased," he continued, "we checked how the militarization of more than 70,000 soldiers obligated the 70,000 families to face death through hunger; we also saw the threat and daily intimidation suffered by the communities. We were witnesses to that. We saw how the soldiers burned and razed the fields, threw the children out of schools, and turned the schools into barracks...And each time we became more familiar with the Zapatistas form of organisation, communal work and cooperation. And I realized that the motives behind the militarization were to break down the community, to keep the people from organizing in an autonomous manner in order to overcome poverty and isolation."

One of the criticisms later levelled at RATM was the fact they endorsed a struggle of Mexican people when there were people in their own country who were poverty stricken and homeless. In their song 'Rage Against The Mac Machine', American hardcore outfit M.O.D. (who were lead by the brash and unashamedly Republican fortnman Billy Milano), sniped, *"Raise a lot of cash and ship it to (Tibet)/You hypocrites, did you forget, there's people starving in our own backyards."*

Yet Mexico *was* part of Zack De La Rocha's make-up, both ancestrally and emotionally, and as a Chicano himself, it was hardly stretching reality to associate himself with the American peoples. Chiapas was as much about his own backyard as Los Angeles.

Again it's a question of knowledge, or rather, a lack of it. When one looks at the statistics for the atrocities happening in Chiapas it makes reasoned action that much more justifiable. Between the mid-Nineties and 2005, 150,000 children in Chiapas died from curable diseases, partially because there are more veterinarians there than there are doctors. There is also only one teacher per thousand children. Only one third of the people have light in their homes despite the fact Chiapas provides 63 percent of the hydro-electric power in the whole of Mexico. Partly due to this and partly due to his affection for the rebel Zapatistas, Zack De La Rocha began an association with the National Commission For Democracy In Mexico, an organisation in place to educate both indigenous and people further afield regarding the Zapatistas and the NAFTA (North American Free Trade Agreement). "Our work here can really save lives," Zack would explain. "The more people who find out about the Zapatistas here, the better the chance of preventing a massive military intervention on behalf of this country."

The Zapatista Army of National Liberation (EZLN) is a self-appointed, self-armed military group based in Chiapas, Mexico. "Chiapas a state rich in resources but poor in standard of living," De La Rocha explains on RATM's *Battle Of Mexico City* DVD. "There are those who will no longer accept the poverty the current system offers them. These people are known as the Zapatistas. Emiliano Zapata Salazar (he dropped the last name) was born August 8, 1879 in Anenecuilco, Morelos, Mexico. At the time, the large property developers were driving out indigenous people and communities. They were forced to either move from their own land or work for those who had taken over their land and resources.

Noted Mexican expert and revered writer, Alan Cogan states, "The hacendados, the fabulously rich landowners, in cahoots with the government, robbed the peasants of their land. The purpose of this outright theft was to turn the land over to sugar cane production, rather than the traditional corn, because sugar at that time brought high prices on world markets. The hacendados lived lives of incredible luxury, spending a great deal of time in European resorts and capitals. They were evidently devoid of pity for the people whose land they stole at the point of a gun, leaving the peasants homeless. A revolution was inevitable."

Zapata would grow to be a revolutionary, campaigning for villagers rights by establishing the people's legal right to the land which was being taken over. Though Zapata was legally correct, the government were slow to act and he decided to create an armed force in response. This force was intended merely to reclaim its own land. The Mexican Revolution of 1910 was a massive uprising in protest at various social and economic conditions and practices and the revolution lasted for almost a decade. Yet, as in many cases in history where a revolutionary creates an unavoidable problem for the government, the powers that be simply remove the offender from their radar. On April 10, 1919, Zapata was invited to a meeting where his opposition claimed to be willing to acquiesce to the villagers. Yet when he arrived he was met with a hail of gunfire from Colonel Guajardo and his men. Or so the story goes. "They say Zapata did not die, he must return," Zack De La Rocha narrates in the *Battle Of Mexico City* DVD.

In the folklore of the people of Morelos, there is an extensive belief that Zapata did not die, that the corpse was that of a friend posing as Zapata, and that Zapata fled to a foreign land where he later died of old age. John Steinbeck, who wrote the screenplay for the superb 1952 biopic of Zapata's life, *Viva Zapata!* (where Zapata was played by Marlon Brando), says in his biography of the man: "Zapata was a greater man than his people. He belongs to the whole world, and his symbol of piracy and violence, and of resistance against oppression, is a world symbol."

In 1994, the Zapatistas declared war against the Mexican state but were soon overpowered by the Mexican army. Since then the group has aimed to seek support from varying factions around the world and used communication and education as their main source of change – if they can enlist the help of thousands around the world they will always have more might than the Mexican army. This is where RATM – or certainly Zack in particular – came in. As Zack had already referenced, the North American Free Trade Agreement is exactly the type of neo-liberal policy the EZLN stand against. The agreement, commonly known as NAFTA, essentially ends the potential for the Mexican people to make their own living.

"What happened as a result of the North American Free Trade Agreement was as it was passed and implemented in Mexico, it nullified article 27 in the Mexican constitution," Zack explained. "Article 27 is the Article which guaranteed land rights to peasants, indigenous farmers, and to their families as a result of what happened in 1910. A million people died in Mexico in the revolution of 1910, and for this very reason, which was nullified by NAFTA, it was a death sentence for the people living down there."

The armed response by the EZLN emanates from a statement made just before the revolt of 1994. The call was to, "demand that the revolutionary armed forces not intervene in matters of civil order or the disposition of capital relating to agriculture, commerce, finances, and industry, as these are the exclusive domain of the civil authorities, elected freely and democratically." In opposition to the influx of violent upheaval, the Zapatistas swore to defend themselves – by any means necessary, as the slogan goes. The statement reads, (that the people should) "acquire and possess arms to defend their persons, families and property, according to the laws of disposition of capital of farms, commerce, finance and industry, against the armed attacks committed by the revolutionary forces or those of the government."

The Zapatista's simply want the right to govern their own people and decide amongst themselves how to use their own land and to live within their own community unfettered by malevolent outside forces. As the EZLN spokesman Subcomandante Marcos has stated on numerous occasions – "My real commander is the people." Marcos is viewed as the leader of the Zapatista's but this has been denied. Instead he prefers to be known simply as a spokesman. He certainly has a huge deal of influence.

Since December 1994, the Zapatistas have successfully made steps to procure their own autonomy and governing system. Several communal programs have been introduced from health and school systems to food-producing programs. Zack felt RATM's music had "become a bridge" to help serve the Zapatistas by making Rage's fans aware of their plight. The singer explained, "It is important for me, as a popular artist, to make clear to the governments of the United States and Mexico that despite the strategy of fear and intimidation to foreigners, despite their weapons, despite their immigration laws and military reserves, they will never be able to isolate the Zapatista communities from the people in the United States."

With reference to the comments made by Billy Milano, there were many statements RATM made concerning their own backyard, from injustice within the prison system to anti-Nazi demonstrations and beyond. Perhaps they could indeed have done more but it was certainly harder to fight the corporatisation of America. Additionally there were plenty of ramifications for Americans concerning the poor treatment of Mexicans.

"Being in Chiapas fills you with a sense of what can really happen in the States if we let it," Zack told Norm Arenas. "America has a mad amount at stake in Mexico. A fourth of all of the oil here comes from Mexico, and they just found oil in Chiapas. What do these communities mean to a government who only serves as a mouthpiece to people like Shell? They mean nothing. These people envision progress through cash-flow reports."

Morello, De La Rocha and Co. were more than aware of the difficulties within their home country, yet Zack was insightful when describing the problem within America. "There are two reasons that the American political culture is as immature as it is," he told *Propaganda*. "The first is the educational system that's been developed to encourage obedience and not critical thinking. The second thing is that the press is pretty extreme to say the least, in the sense that it's the commercial interests that control the US and it isn't interested in letting the kids know what's going on in the country and the world outside. When you hear more about Mike Tyson's life than you do about the 1500 bodies they've found at the border between the US and Mexico in the last five years, you have a serious problem. I think it's those two factors that are responsible for the fact that the US never had a strong political movement."

Such observations were rooted in rationality, but did De La Rocha truly think he could stir a revolution within America? Whether he believed he could or not, the assertion is that any sort of positive change is better than nothing. With Rage Against The Machine providing a vehicle for change and an exchange of information, listeners could then choose as they wished, whether it be buying more books on the real stories behind atrocities and injustices in the world, buying a T-shirt or actually becoming involved with grass roots organisations.

Tellingly, the inner sleeve of *Evil Empire* featured a collage of literature as suggested reading. Notables included *50 Ways To Fight Censorship*, *The Anarchist Cookbook*, *The Black Panthers Speak* and *Race For Justice: Mumia Abu-Jamal's Fight Against The Death Penalty*.

Whether Rage's words inspired actual change, at the very least they were informing listeners, often in a very subliminal way, sometimes in a direct way. Consider the album cover for *Evil Empire* for example. It seems harmless enough, and in fact was the kind of cover record stores and chains were never going to object to stocking but the message was in there whether they knew it or not.

The style of the cover came from the Marvel Comics character Crimebuster, drawn by Mel Ramos 2. There is a clever duality behind the artwork. Firstly there is the literal translation that fits in with the album title itself. The phrase 'Evil Empire' came from the name given to the USSR, yet here Rage were implying that the biggest evil empire is actually the United States and that the likes of Crimebuster needs to start with the biggest evil empire first – the one closest to home, the enemy in the mirror.

Then there is the clandestine snipe at the superhero culture of the comic books, the one which creates fictitious characters who can save the world. Crimebuster was never going to save the world. And the notion that he could is simply a satirical jibe. Should Rage ever lose their musical abilities they could all take up a job running a satirical magazine.

The remaining tracks on *Evil Empire* were harder to digest. It wasn't just a case of needing a few listens to truly get into the material, in some cases it took years. Speaking personally, I did not truly appreciate the genius of the album as a whole until several years after its release despite regularly listening to the entire recording. Perhaps it is because the first album was so instant, so catchy at every venture, and here was an album where you had to work to enjoy it.

In some ways it is easier for a band to write ten catchy songs and make them as instantaneous as possible – this is how pop writers make a living. RATM didn't do obvious or predictable and this is just one reason why their art has not and will not date. Aside from the first two songs, one of the standout tracks, and indeed relatively immediate, was the pistol funk of 'Vietnow'. Upbeat, quirky and about as direct as Rage could get.

"Fear is your only God on the radio," spits De La Rocha, referring to the horrendous mass of prime time popular right-wing radio shows generally found on the AM dial. Here Zack was tackling over-zealous conservative 'political commentators' who support or promote the word of the Lord.

After the thumping 'Revolver' and 'Snakecharmer', which wove its charm and magic through a Commerford bass line wrapped behind the bridge and then chorus, there was the mass of rage that was 'Tire Me', allegedly a song about the death of former president Richard Nixon. And 'Down Rodeo' was a bobbing, weaving nasty slab of souped-up hip-hop.

This was was just one of the songs dealing with life in 'their own backyard'. The lyrics referred to the Rodeo Drive shopping district in Beverly Hills, California, one of the wealthiest shopping areas in the world. Zack's words brimmed with the injustice of poverty within American homes when there are lavish spending sprees going on in an all-white consumer district.

"I have to make sure that this band doesn't become a removed entity from the grassroots," Zack would later say. "When a person's sense of political action rests solely on pulling a ballot box every four years, there's going to be a sense of desperation because it's been proven to fail in bringing about the changes that the working poor need." The song was only released as a promotional single for radio stations etc, but was barely played.

The likes of 'Wind Below' and 'Roll Right' were not the greatest recordings Rage had put their name to and they did somewhat fill out the remainder of the album. Even the closing 'Year Of Tha Boomerang' is less than fervent, though it did ably demonstrate the unusual, off kilter rhythms of Wilk, Commerford and Morello. The latter showed an even greater array of creativity on the guitar throughout the album, changing moods of songs with one scratch here or knob swell there.

"With the second record, I began to feel a creative fulfilment in it," Morello said of his guitar style, and the challenge of moulding it to RATM. "The odd noises had become so much more of a foundation, and I'd try to come up with just crazy, head-turning things. At this point, they're just what I reach for first, the way a blues guitarist would go for a certain tòne and style without having to say, 'Now I'm going to play a blues lick'. The other day, an interviewer claimed that Rage doesn't have a sense of humour. Brad Wilk said, 'You haven't listened to the guitar solos!'"

Evil Empire was released on 15 April, 1996 and went straight in to Number 1 in the American chart, also peaking at Number 4 in the U.K. Rage would go on to win a Grammy for 'Best Metal Performance' with 'Tire Me'. *Kerrang!* awarded the album four out of five K's, admitting, "With such a unique debut tough to equal, Rage played to their strengths and delivered a potent follow-up. 'Bulls On Parade' and 'People Of The Sun' were hits and though *Evil Empire* is arguably even harder in places, they suffered for their own high standards."

Though Tom Morello would assert that *Evil Empire* was a "dark" record and that people didn't necessarily want to hear Rage Against the Machine making a dark album, it seemed to be enough for the fans and critics alike. There were some detractors but the chances are, if anyone spent enough time examining the album, a few years on they would understand it better. For those who expected another 'Killing In The Name'? ... "We just weren't at that spot," Morello responded. "We were in a very dark spot, and it sounds like it."

Still, Rage Against The Machine had silenced the doubters and silenced their own personal doubts. They could function as a unit, even after a few years of questions, worries and second guesses. Not only could they still remain friends, touring partners and band mates, but they could write incendiary, powerful, stirring, anthemic music which could and would change the world.

Chapter Ten
So You Want A Revolution

With the success of *Evil Empire*, Rage Against The Machine had proved they were no one hit wonders. It had taken some time for that second record to come together but they'd made sure the album was immensely strong before releasing it. Now it was time for the band to truly take advantage of their position and increase their activism.

After an appearance on the soundtrack to *Higher Learning*, with 'Year Of Tha Boomerang' (a demo version of 'Tire Me' also appeared in the film), RATM were booked to appear on the American variety show *Saturday Night Live*. Whether the band knew in advance is unclear, but that night the *SNL* guest host was Republican, and then-Presidential candidate, billionaire Steve Forbes. His father Malcolm was the editor-in-chief of business magazine *Forbes* as well as President of its publisher, Forbes Inc.

In protest at Forbes' appearance on the show, given that to RATM he was the embodiment of the right-winger lambasted in 'Vietnow', the band attempted to hang two American flags upside down over their amplifiers seconds before they performed 'Bulls On Parade' – the flags were removed by stage-hands before the statement was broadcast. According to the online RATM fan club, Tom Morello stated the reason for hanging inverted flags was their "contention that American democracy is inverted when what passes for democracy is an electoral choice between two representatives of the privileged class. America's freedom of expression is inverted when you're free to say anything you want to say until it upsets a corporate sponsor." Rage's statement prompted exactly that response.

The producers for *SNL* told the band they'd had to remove the flags in the interest of keeping Forbes happy, that they had to run a "tighter ship" with his appearance. The band was even told that the performance of 'Bullet In The Head' would be censored, with any "objectionable" lyrics being muted.

Through the Rage fan club, Morello intimated that the *SNL* cast and crew, whom he did not name, "expressed solidarity with our actions, and a sense of shame that their show had censored the performance." RATM were incensed and told to leave the building but not before Tim Commerford was alleged to have stormed into Steve Forbes' dressing room and littered it with shreds of one of the flags.

"*SNL* censored Rage, period," explained Tom Morello in the aftermath, on www.esquilax.com. "They could not have sucked up to the billionaire more. The thing that's ironic is *SNL* is supposedly this cutting edge show, but they proved they're bootlickers to their corporate masters when it comes down to it. They're cowards. It should come to no surprise that General Electric would find 'Bullet In The Head' particularly offensive. GE is a major manufacturer of US planes used to commit war crimes in the Gulf War, and bombs from those jets destroyed hydroelectric dams which killed thousands of civilians in Iraq."

Zack had been prompted by Morello before the gig to mention this during 'Bulls On Parade', yet the band's stand could have been so much worse than even *SNL* feared, as Morello later recalled: "If they only had a clue about some of the things we were thinking of doing, they probably would have thanked us for only turning the flags upside down!"

In June 1996, RATM played at the first Tibetan Freedom Concert in Golden Gate Park, San Francisco alongside artists such as Red Hot Chili Peppers, Sonic Youth, De La Soul and Smashing Pumpkins. The idea for the foundation came from Adam Yauch of the Beastie Boys (who also appeared) and took the form of a huge benefit show *a la* Live Aid. Over 100,000 people attended and altogether over $800,000 was raised for Tibetan and social justice causes. "We're playing this show because we oppose oppression in all its forms," Tom Morello would say. "In Tibet now, injustices and violence are perpetrated against people of that region. But what's sometimes forgotten is that prior to the Communist takeover, there were also injustices and violence perpetrated against people, particularly women and the lower classes. It was basically a feudal society. What I think everyone here at the concert wants is self-determination, justice and equality for all the people of Tibet."

Though it was a united front for all musicians, none of whom were paid to play, it was clear that the band with the most powerful delivery was Rage Against The Machine. Morello concurred, "Especially in the US, there needs to be a band like this. If you look at how many bands are singing about getting drunk and having a good time, and I'm not saying that I never get drunk and have a good time, but the ratio of those bands compared to bands that are actually saying something – with full credit to Zack and what he's doing – it's kinda astronomical."

On January 20, 1997, the night of Bill Clinton's inauguration as the next President of the United States, Rage produced a radio show called Radio Free LA, which showcased varying forms of protest and plenty of new, original music. There were interviews and commentary from Public Enemy's Chuck D, film-maker and truth seeker Michael Moore, the Zapatista spokesman Subcomandante Marcos, Noam Chomsky and segments featuring both Leonard Peltier and Mumia Abu Jamal, the latter interviewed from Death Row. These sections were illuminated with music by the likes of Flea, Cypress Hill, Beck and Jane's Addiction's Stephen Perkins. With the latter on drums, Flea on bass and Morello and De La Rocha completing the line-up, the makeshift band performed versions of 'Bulls On Parade', 'Down Rodeo', 'Vietnow' and 'Tire Me'.

Leonard Peltier had been one of RATM's chief causes for some time. At the time of writing, Peltier has been imprisoned for almost 12,000 days, and his supporters claim he is being held illegally. Peltier is a Native American who was born September 12, 1944. He grew up with his grandparents, living on the Turtle Mountain Indian Reservation in North Dakota. Peltier became a member of the American Indian Movement (AIM – a grassroots organization launched in the late Sixties that sparked a resurgence of Indian pride on reservations and in cities throughout America) and his early years were nothing if not peaceful and harmonious. It was only when he was caught up in a fracas in Texas that Peltier's name became synonymous with political imprisonment.

In the early morning hours of November 22, 1972, in a Texas restaurant, it was claimed that Leonard Peltier pointed a Beretta pistol at the stomach of Milwaukee police officer Ron Hlavinka. Peltier supposedly tried to fire the gun twice but neither time succeeded. He was thus tried for attempted murder.

It took two years for police to run a ballistics check on Peltier's Beretta where they discovered it had been inoperable. Five years later Peltier would be acquitted on the attempted murder charge. However the damage had already been done. Peltier was released on bail and left Milwaukee which he was not allowed to do, and promptly became a federal fugitive with a felony warrant following him. At the Jumping Bull Place, on June 26, 1975, two FBI agents, Jack Coler and Ron Williams, were killed in a shootout. Three men were charged for their murders: Bob Robideau, Dino Butler and Leonard Peltier. Both Butler and Robideau were subsequently found to be innocent; yet another court found Peltier guilty and sentenced him to two consecutive life terms.

"You have to understand," Peltier told reporter Scott Anderson, "I didn't kill those agents. I didn't order anyone to kill those agents. I'm an innocent man."

There were a number of inconsistencies regarding the weapon while witness reports conflicted in many cases. Three witnesses testified they saw Peltier approach the slain officers' vehicle. They later said that certain authorities had threatened and forced them to testify. The FBI contested that the witnesses' testimony.

Scott Anderson theorises that the case of Peltier merely highlights "the dramatic rise and fall of the American Indian Movement. AIM, in the view of its supporters, carried the promise of a unified Indian nation, until it was brought down by the heavy-handed tactics of federal law enforcement officials, with Peltier a victim of this larger conspiracy. Did a vengeful Federal Bureau of Investigation, desperate to put someone behind bars for the murder of two of its agents, railroad an innocent man? A great many people think so. Moreover, in locking Peltier away for life, did the government orchestrate yet another miscarriage of justice in its checkered (sic) relationship with American Indians?"

It was not just Rage Against The Machine who have lent their support to the Peltier cause. Many other musicians including Robbie Robertson to Ben Harper have also spoken out and defended Peltier. Yet perhaps most revealingly there have also been a huge number of high profile celebrity and political names who gave their signature to an official letter/petition of support for Peltier. These included Mikhail Gorbachev and Desmond Tutu as well as many other famous singers such as Madonna and Bono.

The re-election of Bill Clinton featured one of the lowest turnouts in American political history. Whether it was apathy or the realisation that their vote wouldn't change a thing, it started an ongoing denial of the system by many Americans, particularly young voters. According to Morello, "Radio Free LA provided a musical and political gathering point for the majority of Americans, and young people especially, who rightly felt left out of the 'democratic process'." Over 50 commercial radio stations broadcast the show simultaneously and the official RATM website also carried the full show as a live stream.

In an unexpected move, Rage teamed up with rock giants U2 in April 1997 for their PopMart tour. For this show, all RATM's profits went to various organisations, such as Women Alive (an organisation to support women living with HIV and A.I.D.S.), U.N.I.T.E. (a British/Irish trade union) and the Zapatista Front For National Liberation.

In August, Rage went in a very different direction, choosing Wu-Tang Clan as their touring partners for a US jaunt. After just a week of shows however, the Wu-Tang dropped off the tour. They were replaced by bands including Roots and Foo Fighters. The reason for Wu-Tang Clan leaving the tour was never fully explained but it seemed to be internal conflicts within the band. As Tom Morello would acknowledge, "It's hard enough when you've got a band with four people. Imagine one with nine plus, or however many in it. But we got along great on the road. We had the opportunity to jam four or five nights at the end of shows, songs with RZA, Method Man, and Raekwon. It was really cool, it was great being on tour with them, and I would have loved to have done the whole tour."

There were other factors which probably did not help matters.

In numerous states local police tried unsuccessfully to cancel the concerts. In Washington they claimed that both bands had "violent and anti-law enforcement philosophies." The *Seattle Times* reported the incident and reasoned RATM's boycott was for "a group known nationally for its politically charged performances."

Clearly, Rage were getting under the skin of the establishment, something they found distinctly satisfying. Even when they weren't in a particular state, the States were still trying to subvert their actions. A sheriff in Colorado was found to be sending out memorandums to other promoters and venues warning them of the "dangerous" Rage Against The Machine. Tom Morello was indignant, elaborating that it, "was highlighted in the police memorandum that it was Rage's anti-police, anti-authority position that they were fearing was going to incite kids, and that they had witnessed this behaviour at a number of different shows, which means that there is a de facto police monitoring of music in this country. And that there is a network to inform police departments and venues around the country when a rock tour is found to have objectionable lyrics."

Still, this kind of incitement was exactly what the band was about as Zack De La Rocha later stated. "We're not playing Spice Girls songs," he cracked. "I feel the same kind of passion – perhaps passion's not the right word – the same kind of *fury* that you might feel in a confrontation, at a demonstration with the cops. In our best moments."

By now, De La Rocha was even more fervently against the protocols of mainstream rock music, having had his trust abused by various journalists. Even in the early days he had decided to let his lyrics speak for themselves, preferring to expand upon those particular topics rather than his favourite colour or similar such such vacuous subjects. After all, he was here for only one thing and talking about pointless or personal subjects was just not going to accomplish much. Eventually, come the end of 1996, he would decline any interviews which did not focus on topics he wanted to talk about, specifically the Zapatista movement.

By refusing to talk about anything except his own specifics, Zack argued he was protecting the band's integrity. He told Ben Myers in 1999 that, "It's important that artists in my position set an example and there's a fine line between the promotion of a product and the promotion of an idea. And so, to protect my integrity, I decided to refrain."

The final straw came when during an interview for a UK magazine, one particular unnamed journalist asked Zack to speak about his father. When the singer declined on the basis he didn't want it to go in print, the journalist promised it would just be between the two of them. De La Rocha took him at his word but as Zack told Norm Areans, "he had a wire. He printed everything. If I see him now, I'm gonna fucking kill the guy."

So De La Rocha chose to live through the intensity of his band's music and his poetic verse, words which no one could distort or use against him. And in a live setting, the band simply exploded. It wasn't just the vocalist who spewed into some sort of demonic concoction, the entire troupe were united and precise.

When outside interference messed with the band they were even more untouchable, as Brad Wilk would tell *Kerrang!* when he referenced a show they played in the small area of Kristiana within Copenhagen, Denmark in 1996. This area of Copenhagen is essentially a glorified squat, converted from an old army barracks, a communal area for varying clusters of the poor or alternatively minded.

"It was the most intense moment of my career," he recalled. "We were tear-gassed on our bus right before we were due to go onstage. I remember the police coming in and trying to incite a riot, even though the kids weren't doing anything. After it happened we got up and played the most intense show we've ever done. After being threatened like that, I have never felt so alive in my life."

In 1997, RATM joined up with Snoop Dogg (then known as Snoop Doggy Dogg) to create a track, which was used on his 'Doggfather' single. The song was 'Snoop Bounce' and was fun to make, as Tim Commerford told Ben Myers.

"It was a cool-ass song," said the bassist. "It had Charlie Wilson from The Gap Band singing some of the vocals. We spent a couple of days writing the song, recorded it, then called up Snoop to come on down. Charlie Wilson did his weird shit then Snoop Dogg came in and fucking went off, laid it down, one take.

He smoked a lot of dope, brought a lot of people, turned off all the lights then ... boom! He went off. Snoop Dogg's got skills, definitely. He's got style."

In the same year, Rage celebrated their dominance on stage with a video release featuring various live performances and all their videos to date, in full, uncensored glory. It was actually a first for the US to release these videos in their unhampered form, up until then, no one had been brave enough to show the full unexpurgated versions of the likes of 'Killing In The Name' or 'People Of The Sun'. There was also an additional treat on the video, the studio version of a song RATM had been playing all summer long – Bruce Springsteen's 'The Ghost Of Tom Joad'.

Perhaps it was inevitable Rage would identify with a blue collar 'man of the people' artist like Bruce Springsteen, even though many of the members had grown up without any interest in the man known as 'The Boss'. Here was a multi-millionaire rock star who managed to retain his integrity, singing of social causes and being involved in progressive politics at the same time as being on a corporate major label (Columbia). It was ironic an artist such as Springsteen had indeed maintained credibility where a band like Rage, after just two albums, were being criticised for their apparent hypocrisy. After all, Springsteen was not so deeply involved with grass roots politics and had released enough records to keep himself solvent for several lifetimes. Moreover he was also a staunch patriot, eager to sing for the positive aspects of America and being an American.

Springsteen carefully balanced the understated protest songs and melancholy reflections with rock anthems which became a jingoistic symbol. His 1984 album *Born In The USA* was the definition of small town patriotism and belief in the American dream. The cover even featured a backdrop of the American flag (and it wasn't upside down). However, the lyrics were actually an opposing statement to nationalism and concerned the return of American Vietnam war soldiers. Like RATM with their covert references and sometimes ambiguous topics, Springsteen seemed to have the last laugh.

"They put a rifle in my hands," comes the refrain from this most mainstream of pop songs, "sent me off to Vietnam, to go and kill the yellow man." It's amazing how a song which pumps with an upbeat keyboard riff, and a seemingly innocuous song title, can convince the moral majority it's a patriotic rallying cry. The song was even praised by President Ronald Reagan as a symbol of being a good, all-American anthem.

"When I was in high school, when I had friends who said they were going to see him I'd say, 'Are you out of your mind? All that money and he's not even heavy metal?'" Morello told Jane Ganahl regarding Springsteen. "And I went through an anti-Bruce phase when 'Born In The USA' was popular, because I hadn't really listened to the words and there were some songs that were really syrupy sweet and I thought, 'That is really whack-ass shit'. But then he was on HBO or something doing an Amnesty International concert from Brazil, and I couldn't believe what I saw. It was so moving. And there were 200,000 people there and it was like he controlled the crowd with all the intensity of, like a small Jane's Addiction show. So I had to go out and buy his albums."

Tim Commerford had exactly the same perception of The Boss. "When I was a kid I was like 'Bruce Springsteens's a goof-ball, man, I'm not into him!'" he laughingly remembered. "I wouldn't cut the guy any slack. I was just like, 'It better be rocking or I don't want to hear it!' Since playing 'The Ghost Of Tom Joad' night after night, I've reconsidered my opinions on Bruce Springsteen and I'm like 'Wow, that guy is a voice of a generation, he's a voice of the working-class'."

For Rage Against The Machine, their goal was to continue to push the boundaries and to this end they began to crusade against sweatshop labour both domestically and in countries such as India. They focussed on the Guess? fashion emporium, who is criticised for allegedly using poor labour conditions and flouting the minimum wage guarantee. Through RATM's campaigning there were several billboards, featuring a photo of the band, placed throughout New York and Las Vegas reading, "Rage Against Sweatshops: We Don't Wear Guess? – A Message from Rage Against The Machine and UNITE."

Tom Morello illuminated to *Guitar World*, "America touts itself as the land of the free, but the number one freedom that you and

I have is the freedom to enter into a subservient role in the workplace. Once you exercise this freedom, you've lost all control over what you do, what is produced, and how it is produced. And in the end, the product doesn't belong to you. The only way you can avoid bosses and jobs is if you don't care about making a living. Which leads to the second freedom: the freedom to starve."

Such was Morello's commitment that he was arrested in December 1997 for his part in a demonstration in Santa Monica, California, where he and several co-protesters were simply raising awareness of the practices of Guess? "It was a good day's work," he said. "Break into the shopping mall, block the Robinsons May Store, get arrested, spend the day in jail. Still the end result did generate a lot of press, and the boycott was successful."

Soon Rage Against The Machine would be most identifiable as the chief supporters of the imprisoned writer and poet Mumia Abu-Jamal. A Pennsylvania governor signed the death warrant for Abu-Jamal in 1995 and it was here that RATM stepped in to offer support. Their backing was not limited to the case itself however; to them it was just as much about the death penalty as a punishment. Working directly with the Jamal case they were serving a dual purpose – to hopefully see his release and to use a high profile case to alert people to the unfairness of a death sentence. After all, what if the person convicted were innocent? Shouldn't there be a hundred percent certainty, from DNA evidence, that the person was guilty of the crime? And even then, where should the line be drawn as to what constitutes an offence which is punishable by death? Yet even if this were to be acceptable, in the case of Mumia Abu Jamal the evidence was less than convincing. As Tom Morello would say, "Anyone with a surface understanding of the case knows that there's a lot of funny business going on."

Born Wesley Cook in 1954, Abu Jamal grew up in Philadelphia, Pennsylvania. He became a Black Panther activist in his early teens and was also a writer. He was well known to the authorities as a subservive political commentator, speaking out against police brutality and varying injustices through reports on local radio stations.

To supplement his income he drove a cab through the night and one particular, fateful evening in 1981 he had just dropped off a passenger when he heard gunshots nearby. When he came to the scene he found his brother, street vendor, William Cook staggering in the street. As Mumia left his cab to attend to his brother he was shot by a police officer and dropped to the ground, only half-conscious. A few minutes later further police arrived on the scene and found the officer dead, Abu-Jamal was still breathing. He was arrested and allegedly beaten before being driven to a hospital, which took over 30 minutes despite it being only a five minute drive. Abu-Jamal survived but was to be tried for the murder of the policeman, Daniel Faulkner. The omens were not good for Mumia. The judge presiding over the case held the record for the most people sent to death row, a dubious distinction which led to his nickname of 'Prosecutor In Robes'.

To his supporters, the trial of Abu-Jamal was a farce from the outset. Jury members were seemingly haphazardly selected and he was accused of disrupting court proceedings leading to an outside choice of attorney. Mumia could not even attend most of his trial due to red tape and the assertion he was sabotaging proceedings. Crucially the jury was devoid of any African-Americans.

There were several conflicting scraps of evidence, chiefly that the weapon Mumia legally owned, a .38 calibre weapon, was used in the shooting. Despite this declaration from the prosecution, the bullet removed from Faulkner's brain was actually from a .44 calibre, though the jury were not told this. At the scene of the crime Abu-Jamal was not even searched to check for powder residue from the gun, nor was the gun tested to see if it had been fired a moment before.

The jury were told Mumia had confessed to the murder, while he was at the hospital. Yet in the police officer's report made just after the conversation he noted that "the negro made no comments." Additionally the doctor who was tending to Mumia the whole time contested he did not hear him speak at all.

Some prosecution witnesses were accused of being police informants and others came forward to add that police intimidation of witnesses was present. Another small fact which did not emerge until thirteen years after the initial trial was that there was a driving license belonging to another male which was found on top of Daniel Faulkner's body. There were ten witnesses altogether that were at the scene and five of those suggested at least one man ran from the scene.

Mumia Abu-Jamal was found guilty and sentenced to death; many believed his political beliefs and outspokenness was the reason rather than the murder. Every single appeal which has been lodged has been denied, there seems to be no possibility of a retrial and it seems likely Mumia will either die in prison or by lethal injection.

"He had a spotless police record at the time of the incident," Morello says of Mumia. "The one thing he has always been guilty of is that he's been a leading critic of police violence against minority communities. His outspoken opposition to racism and police brutality is what we believe got him in trouble and made him a marked man. For many years on Death Row he continues to not beg for his life, but to courageously deliver scathing social criticism, like his book *Live From Death Row* and his commentaries on both domestic and international events. He's probably the most censored man in America."

Rage Against The Machine have contributed considerable efforts and funds to the appeals process for Abu-Jamal and continue to support this most controversial of cases.

Chapter Eleven
Killing Pretenders

In June of 1998, Sony released a B-Sides and live compilation of RATM material titled *Live & Rare*. It was the first opportunity the band had to pay homage to their influences and push the boundaries on their art. As well as the expected inclusion of now firmly established live greats such as 'Take The Power Back' and 'Bullet In The Head', the band lined up an interesting collage of extra material. There was their paean to the reactionary protest poet Allen Ginsberg with his 'Hadda Be Played On The Jukebox' rant – an incisive view of government and society. Originally a pure poem, Rage set a repetitive bass and drums backdrop, with occasional guitar feedback flourishes, while De La Rocha gradually increased his venom, building up to the natural crescendo of the poem. Unlike some of his other vocals, here he made sure to enunciate every word as clearly as possible – a relatively unremarkable piece of music made captivating by the frontman's vocal delivery.

"We wanted to just quickly send a nice quiet message to the fraternal order of police in Philadelphia, here's something nice and friendly…" said De La Rocha by way of introduction to the N.W.A. classic 'Fuck The Police'. The band kicked in with a funky backdrop, paying homage to one of the most subversive artists of all-time. The cover version was faithful to the original, laying little into the arrangement or extras and digging straight into the basic beat and repeating the lyrics verbatim. The sentiment was the most important thing.

A much underrated Rage song is their contribution to *The Crow* soundtrack, with 'Darkness'. The compilation was one of the first successful combinations of heavy metal, punk and alternative bands, including Stone Temple Pilots, Helmet, Nine Inch Nails, Pantera, The Cure and Jesus & Mary Chain. Somehow it all melded together perfectly. Rage's song had little in common with the gothic themes of the film, though musically the flowing, eerie bass and guitar lines fit the dark, twisted scenes, while the lyrics concerned the plight of the African and Mexican people referring especially to the control of indigenous land and the introduction of diseases such as AIDS.

'Clear The Lane' was a demo track from before *Rage Against The Machine* and must rate as one of RATM's most unusual tracks, abnormal in its simplicity and an almost naïve approach to rap rock. Yet for this fledgling style, the power is palpable and it rates as one of Rage's most enjoyable tracks. Sounding somewhat thinner than their work on the debut album, it nevertheless packs a punch with the bravado of rap culture – from underlining their authenticity to name-checking a band member with a reference to "Timmy C".

The album passed by relatively unnoticed but was a stronger accompaniment to the Rage manifesto and only pressed home their authenticity and ground breaking approach. It was also a nice touch to include the soundtrack recording on *Live & Rare* to save people buying *The Crow* just to hear one RATM track.

During the band's tour of 1993 as they pulled into the New Orleans stop on the Lollapalooza stint, Tim and Brad were both arrested after Tim stepped into question police as they searched a homeless black man. Though Commerford vehemently claimed he was sober, he was arrested on a charge of 'public intoxication'.

"The only thing the experience did for me is to make me realise I seriously cannot stand police at all," he told *Spin* magazine. "I'm going to vocalise to any cop I ever see that I hate him and wish he was dead, based solely on the fact that he's a cop. I promise you that one day, maybe it'll be ten years from now, I'll go, 'I'm even with the police'. I'll go, 'I can't tell you what I did, but I can tell you that I'm even.'" The day after Tim's arrest, Mary Morello walked onstage to introduced Rage and led the crowd in a chant of "Fuck the New Orleans police!"

The release of RATM's first live material evoked memories of the early Rage days where drummer Brad Wilk would play with his back to the audience out of shyness. One particular occasion where the drummer sat facing the wall led to a somewhat ridiculous incident however. During a gig at the Hollywood Palladium while the band were performing 'Bullet In The Head', Tom Morello's guitar power completely cut off leaving him standing there with nothing to do as the song built to a climax. Instead of sheepishly waltzing off or pretending he didn't realise, Morello jumped up onto Wilk's drum riser to thump a cymbal in defiance. It was Wilk who was primed to thump however, as he wrongly assumed Morello was attacking him and turned to fight his guitarist! The song faltered and then stopped with the crowd watching in amazement, along with their bandmates Zack and Tim who stood agog at the situation.

That same year Tom Morello teamed up with the Prodigy's Liam Howlett to record a song called 'One Man Army' for the movie soundtrack *Spawn*. "I just came up with a bunch of grooves and noises and sent them over to Liam," said Morello, "and had him cut them up, and then he sent them back to me, and we talked. We arranged a song over the phone while we were both on tour."

It became Morello's favourite collaboration with any outside artist. "It was awesome," the guitarist later said. "That's the non-Rage song I'm probably most proud of because basically what Liam did as the person who assembled it was put together a Prodigy-esque song entirely from my guitar playing, as opposed to going down the normal sampling route."

Perhaps Morello's enthusiasm and enjoyment stemmed from the fact this was more like a Prodigy track than anything Rage's guitarist had previously put his name to. Though there were the noticeable six string glitches and noises, it wouldn't have been instantly identifiable as a Tom Morello track unless you already knew.

The live RATM extravaganza ploughed on, playing shows all over the world and stirring action wherever they went. There were some who only liked the band's music and either weren't interested or didn't care about the politics, which was just fine by the band. Morello even said, "The people who just come for the rock, I've never seen that as a downside. We don't play music that is for intellectuals in coffeehouses, you know? We're a tremendously visceral, rocking band."

This was the reason the band had established and maintained such a broad fan base. They did not discredit or alienate anyone who did not follow their causes. It was simply a case of providing the information and letting the individual do what they wanted with it. This was not some cult, or straight edge community where you were frowned upon for not endorsing each and every facet of the behavioural rules. There was an unwritten rule of respect for each other and respect for others, something which RATM detractors would have done well to adhere to. The band would elucidate whenever requested that their causes created a lot of positive change, whether it be reading more deeply into the issues they mentioned or even going so far as to campaign against issues directly: starting an underground fanzine, starting a website, raising money or writing to the government. Rage started to see the numbers of people involved with groups such as the Anti Nazi League increase, no doubt partly due to the band's endorsement.

Certain magazines would push the notion that a lot of RATM's gigs were only about kids moshing or hurting each other – despite the groups' denial. In July 1999, RATM played at the Woodstock festival which had found a relative resurgence based on the original peace and love festival of 1969. This time it was no such peaceful occasion however.

Plagued with problems from the start, the festival would eventually become known for several unsavoury incidents. Writing in the *National Review*, Christopher Caldwell explained, "A frat-boy-saturated crowd groped and perhaps raped a number of the bare-breasted girls being passed over the mosh pit and, once the music had stopped, emptied a couple of 18-wheelers full of souvenirs and smashed a handful of automatic teller machines."

The weather was stifling yet no one was allowed to bring their own food or drink into the venue and small bottles of water were selling within the grounds for between $5 and $8. No water was given out to members of the crowd during any of the bands' sets and people became dehydrated and tense.

"When you have a show and it's 100 degrees out, and when people are coming in and you're taking water away, which they did do, and when you force them to buy an $8 bottle of water, you're going to have problems," Tim Commerford said afterwards. "By the time we got onstage there were kids screaming for water. So that was the problem, and I don't care what anyone says about the music or the testosterone or the country or whatever. It was water. It came down to that. You take water away from people in 100-degree weather, they're going to riot. There's no two ways about it."

It didn't help that one particular band, rap rockers Limp Bizkit, hyped up the crowd during their set. One of their best known songs, 'Break Stuff' felt like an anthem and frontman Fred Durst did little to convince the crowd not to smash anything and everything in sight, something the disgruntled, dehydrated fans had no problem doing. Rage hated playing the show. The sexual assaults and the mindless violence were the complete antithesis of the original Woodstock and didn't feel too good in 1999. The media shit storm that followed only made matters worse.

"I thought the media coverage was grossly unfair and youth-bashing and tried to vilify an entire generation because of a couple of idiots there," Tom Morello reflected on MTV. "And I thought it was ridiculous how they were saying it was this horribly violent event that was a betrayal of the principles of Woodstock. When everyday, whether it's police murders of unarmed citizens or President Clinton's Tomahawk missiles blowing up children's hospitals outside of Belgrade, there are acts of real violence, that are real betrayals of principles, which get one-tenth of the column inches."

The advent of the recent Woodstock had provided another point of reference – that of rap rock or rap metal. Here were Rage Against The Machine sharing a bill with the likes of Limp Bizkit, Kid Rock and Korn, all of whom had found success in Rage's wake. The difference was here was a bunch of white rappers who were, to their many critics, cashing in on the success of the rap metal movement kick-started by Ice T and Co. and furthered by RATM. At least Korn were relatively original with unusual guitar sounds and an innovative approach. Limp Bizkit however had found fame after a cover of George Michael's 'Faith' and proceeded to milk that success over several further, increasingly awful albums.

"For every Nirvana there were 10 or 15 Bush's or whoever," De La Rocha quipped, "and with Rage Against The Machine there's been some not so great bands." "It's interesting to me that back in 1992 we were doing it and now there's just the surgance (sic) of this music in mainstream," Tom Morello pondered, "but I think a lot of it is missing musically and the messages aren't really hitting like we are. "

Zack De La Rocha rightly concurred, "I haven't seen anyone, musically, that has fused it as tastefully as we have and provided it with such a strong backdrop for what we're gonna be doing and what we want to get done. I think we can bridge the gap between entertainment and activism first and foremost, that's our goal. Musically I haven't seen anyone who has fused it as well and I'm waiting, I'm not saying that just to fucking blow my horn, I'm saying it because I haven't seen it. But there'll be others hopefully that can use the space that we created – we encourage it."

It didn't seem RATM were in any danger of having their position at the top of the rap rock tree overtaken. The irony was that they were not influencing any other black rap rock artists to come out of the background. In the Eighties, Living Colour spawned many a black rock band to start up, gradually forming a whole new exciting and colourful scene, yet the Nineties saw very little inspiring material from any cross-over black artists. Whether this was simply because they weren't forming, or they were ignored by record companies is unknown but it would have been interesting for similar minded bands with their roots in white and black music to come along and challenge Rage. Perhaps they just knew there was going to be no competing with the likes of Morello and De La Rocha.

Chapter Twelve
Lost Angeles

In 1998, Rage appeared with a brand new song on the soundtrack to the *Godzilla* movie. 'No Shelter' was about as far removed as it could be from the other acts on the record and the whole vibe of such a mainstream product. This was an album that featured the likes of pop punks Green Day, alternative darlings Foo Fighters and lethargic rapper Puff Daddy. Yet here was RATM with a song typically furious and dissident. Once again Rage were manipulating the machine from the inside, De La Rocha spitting, "Godzilla pure motherfuckin' filler, Get your eyes off the real killer," apparently in a jibe against the very film the band was appearing in!

In general 'No Shelter' focuses on the faux rebellion of designer labels, the persistence of war and the fact that at the very height of conflict – for instance Vietnam – the likes of Coca Cola was still readily available and even provided to those on the front line. The songs included some of Zack's most powerful and poetic lyrics to date. The video was just as powerful, featuring 1920s style scenes of workers on factory floors, whilst the band played in an abandoned warehouse setting.

Given the tag line to the *Godzilla* movie was, 'Size Does Matter', Rage paraphrased at every opportunity to have subliminal digs at the futility of the film and make their own points. For instance, during scenes of the video which are in city streets there are billboards with messages such as, 'Justice Does Matter' when referring to Mumia Abu-Jamal with an empty cell. A huge building is adorned with the slogan, 'Babies born into poverty in the US each year would fill this building – inequality does matter!'

Then there was a reference to the indigenous people of Mexico with the banner 'Land stolen from Mexico equals five states – imperialism matters!' The area from California to Texas was highlighted to show the extent of the theft.

As 1999 dawned, it was time for Rage Against The Machine to think about a new studio album. It had been over three years since *Evil Empire* and with their next album – to be called *The Battle Of Los Angeles* – Rage sought to turn a corner. "I can't say that any of us were necessarily disappointed with the record," Morello said of *Evil Empire*, "but I think we've kinda come full circle with this [new] record and made it for all the right reasons. And I can hear it; it's just so much broader than *Evil Empire*. That was so dark, I think that this record is definitely more upbeat and it has anger, but there are emotions of hope as well and I think we felt a lot better about doing this, and more confident going into it, and all of us were in real good place with each other."

The positivism showed – the album was indeed more upbeat and buzzed with a broader unity, you could almost feel the band bouncing off each other as in the early days. "There's a greater solidarity in the band which grew out of making this record," Morello explained, "because it really gave us the opportunity to become friends again." Yet, the incisiveness of the material still meant that this was not going to be anything other than a pure RATM record full of heartfelt causes, political strife and resident anger.

This was the first time the band could relax while still creating incendiary material. Though the cliché of a band's difficult third album applied by default, it seemed to make no odds to Rage Against The Machine. If anything they were even more relaxed about it. They all made a pact not to go overboard with lengthy sessions and specifically made time to chill out. There was a lot of touch football (a less physical version of the real thing, with no vicious tackling) all of which was filmed and then watched back in slow motion to everyone's amusement. "It was the hardest I'd laughed in years," joked Tim Commerford.

The perennial joker Brendan O'Brien, who was overseeing his second Rage album, was part of the good time vibe and he joined in with the band in every stage of goofing around. Still, as was his specialty, when it came to pressing 'Record' and releasing the band's talent, creativity and beauty, O'Brien was right on the button. Still he felt his job went beyond the demands of the studio, saying, "Making records with Rage Against The Machine is definitely some of the more challenging work I've done, although not necessarily the recording because, well, let's face the reality: it's a guitar, bass, drums, and a guy singing. Seriously, how hard can that be? But honestly, sometimes it's like whatever I can do to make those four guys just communicate with each other, that's what my gig is."

Both O'Brien and the band felt it was necessary to push the boundaries of their recording techniques even further. So, although they were still a live band with no samples or outside additions, they tried every type of effect, sound and static they could possibly create with their instruments (some even fretless), effects pedals and amps. It made the album more rounded than they had ever managed before. They sounded like a fuller rock band at the same time as a more direct hip-hop outfit. There were greater nods to reflective influences, whether it be the background reggae vibes on 'Mic Check', the background funk of 'Maria' or the computer game squeals in the background to 'Voice Of The Voiceless'.

"There's one song where you'd swear we used a sample," Morello said of 'Sleep Now In The Fire', "but I was just doing guitar overdubs, and in the middle of the take, every time I clicked off my distortion pedal, this crazy Korean radio station would start coming out of my little Music Man amp. We heard that back and we were like, 'That's staying!' You'd think it was some sort of researched sample of an old Korean record or something, but we can still say it was all performed live."

The Battle Of Los Angeles was RATM's most ambitious effort to date. It was now expected and accepted that Rage didn't make instant records. Though there were spots of instant gratification, especially the singles 'Sleep Now In The Fire' and 'Guerrilla Radio', the remainder of the album would take on a new dimension upon every listen, gradually increasing its enjoyment over the months and years of existence. This was a difficult task. Was it merely because any song can become admirable after multiple open-minded listens or was it genuinely because Rage had weaved a magic tapestry which gently expanded through time? It was probably a mixture of both, but there is no doubt the band planned the subliminal assaults behind a lot of the tracks and didn't take the easy option of writing twelve tracks which all followed the pattern of 'Guerrilla Radio' or something successful from the past. We weren't going to hear 'Killing In The Name' Part 2, or 'Bulls On Parade' over and over again and that was where Rage's true creative chemistry emerged. They didn't need to rewrite those types of songs because they had enough ideas and means to execute them to make sure they continued to expand the lines of their art.

Still, there were constants to every Rage album. There would be upbeat sing-a-long tracks which resonated in the brain after the very first listen (both singles again), and those songs which carried a more personal tenure and built to emotion teasing crescendos ('Born Of A Broken Man') and then the other tracks which would all carry their own inimitable style and reveal something new over time (see everything else).

The band would also continue their tradition of lending their most revolutionary lyrics to the most buoyant tracks, leading to the inevitable conclusion that radio would play these songs probably without realising what the band were singing about, a trait their respected associate Bruce Springsteen enjoyed with 'Born In The USA'.

The Battle Of Los Angeles melded the entire spectrum of the band's influences with their own creativity, poetry and the inevitable additional noises. The band were unanimous that this was their strongest record to date, a far cry from their almost apologetic and withdrawn reaction regarding *Evil Empire*.

"It's got the anger from the best punk rock, the deepest funk from the best hip-hop and it's something that we're tremendously proud of," Tom Morello beamed in *Kerrang!*. "I still get the same kick that I got when I put on a Kiss record when I was 16 as I do from Rage. I've played with many different musicians and with many other bands, and there is nothing that comes close to Rage."

This rang true for the fans as much as the group. Not only were RATM instantly identifiable, they were unlike any other band.

Hell, even each one of their albums was vastly different from the others. Track to track they could transfer rage or melancholy in one single measure, coming on like Public Enemy in one bar and a modern Led Zeppelin in another. Somehow, through all this diversity, the band held a coherent sound together and managed to make their material interesting, changeable and best of all, built to last.

The progression of the musicians was palpable on the album, most notably the genre defying rhythms of Brad Wilk. "One of my biggest assets is being able to put together completely different grooves and make them sound good and interesting together," he told one drum magazine. "Straight grooves with funky grooves or whatever. With our band, it's rare that there's a song that has just one feel."

For the drummer it was a case of 'less is more'. "I just wasn't concerned with elaborate fills for transitions," he told *DRUM!* magazine. "As a matter of fact I was more interested in building tension from the lack thereof, and putting the intensity into one or two hits. While I was recording this record, I was listening to a lot of Keith Moon's playing, and trying to take his excitement and his spirit and then use it in one or two beats."

Wilk was also part of the solution with regards to band unity, a persistent positive thinker who tended to joke around more than the others. It was he who was responsible for one of the great one liners regarding the band's unabated political stance. "We don't wake up in the morning and rage against the milk carton because we can't get it open," he told Ben Myers.

And so Rage Against The Machine's third album started with the mighty slab of funk that was 'Testify'. This was a damning condemnation of the price of politics – whether it be wars for oil or the media slant on reasons for war, or the fact that there is an extremely narrow choice in candidates (and the things they represent) for the people to elect.

Zack referenced George Orwell's satirical novel *1984* which was perhaps the first time we were told that 'Big Brother' was watching us. Orwell was a satirist by trade and without question he knew of the bigger picture behind the institutions ruling our every day lives. The video to 'Testify' was directed by modern political satirist Michael Moore and contained images of seemingly unconnected individuals who have been reputed as members of the Illuminati, from George Herbert Walker Bush to Pope John Paul II. Most obviously the video makes reference to the lack of choice for voters with a mutant George W. Bush and Al Gore morphing together (these were the two 'choices' for the US presidential election of 2000).

"The one thing the right wing definitely has together is their propaganda machinery," Tom would tell www.morphizm.com. "They've got several TV networks pumping out scandalous disinformation 24 hours a day about what's going on in the world. I'm sure you've seen the statistics that show that the more you watch *Fox News*, the *less* you actually know about what's going on around you. Everything from weapons of mass destruction to the non-link between Saddam and Al-Qaeda, you're likelier to be stupid after watching *Fox News* than if you watched no news at all. That's just one of the elements."

Second track 'Guerrilla Radio' crashed in with a military drumbeat before breaking down into a gorgeous slab of riotous funk, perforated by a creeping, high funk bassline courtesy of Commerford, as De La Rocha rapped over the beats. The song dealt with the ongoing Mumia Abu-Jamal saga as well as the Gore/Bush debacle, screaming for change and the ability to effect it. There are indeed references to Rage's own work and the song essentially called for greater swathes of this kind of propaganda. The parting line was a stirring blast of dedication: "All hell can't stop us now." The song was to become the most identifiable on the album, and became the next Rage anthem, following on from 'Killing In The Name' and 'Bulls On Parade'. Every album needs a focal point and this was [the one on] *The Battle Of Los Angeles*. Such was its impact, the band were again awarded with a Grammy, this time for 'Best Hard Rock Performance'.

It was an obvious choice for first single as Tim Commerford explained: "That was one area where we let Sony, or Epic, get involved with the record. We have complete creative control over everything we do, but occasionally, when we make a record, we'll ask the people that put 'em out and promote 'em, 'What's your favourite song?' And it was unanimous that that was the one. Then there was a few of us trying to bring up other songs that we maybe liked better, but at the end of the day it just came back to that song. And then Zack had to change the lyrics. There was an original version that was a little bit more off-the-cuff lyrically. I thought it was great, but Zack wasn't happy with it, and so he went back and re-recorded the lyrics." In the video itself, the sweatshop workers were real union members from the Garment Workers' Union.

There then came the purposeful, monolithic sound of 'Calm Like A Bomb' (featuring "some of Zack's best lyrics that he's ever written", according to Morello) and the clearest paean to pure hip-hop RATM yet emitted with 'Mic Check'. Tim Commerford explained the stronger veer towards straight hip-hop vibes, saying, "There were drastic differences in musical tastes in the band at the time of *Evil Empire*, but we've come around. It used to be kind of a war between hip-hop and metal. And then I have to bring up the punk side of it too. The punk was the one we all agreed on. We wanted to be a punk band, but we wanted to play some heavy music and we wanted to play hip-hop too. It was kind of unsaid, but I felt the battle. Now hip-hop is bigger than it's ever been, and we're all more into it than we've ever been, so the hip-hop side of the music has definitely come through more on this album."

'Sleep Now In The Fire' was another album highlight. Beginning with a typically impassioned, high key riff, the song broke down into a torrent of ride cymbals and tapped snare drum before eliciting the mighty chorus as the guitars kicked in to full effect. Lyrically the song was a mish-mash of varying observations, from the bombing of Hiroshima to the Agent Orange (chemical warfare) used in the Vietnam War. The song title in fact was a reference to the bombing and subsequent explosions which have killed billions of people across the various wars waged by the United States. It brought back images of the burning monk on the cover of the debut album.

"'Sleep Now In The Fire' was written during a break that we took after the aborted attempt to make *Evil Empire*," Morello told Ben Myers. "I was jamming with friends and immediately stopped the rehearsal and got out my little tape recorder because I remember thinking 'This one might be special ...' You can say what you want about me but you can't say I'm not stubborn so years later when we came to *The Battle Of Los Angeles* session, it was one that I insisted that we work on – over some objection, I should add. It's one of my favourite songs and something that all four of us agreed was a pretty great jam. It combines that big riff with a Seventies funk/soul bass line and a really great lyric. I think the working title of this song was 'MC5'."

The song featured a video which was again directed by Michael Moore and created one of the biggest stirs a popular band could cause when the touted filming of the video, outside the New York Stock Exchange, caused the insiders to shut it down for fear of crowds spilling in and causing mayhem. The band had obtained a federal permit which allowed them to perform on the grounds of the building located inches from Wall Street but Moore still managed to be threatened with police arrest and was detained for an hour. Though it was a shame the building did not get stormed with angry youths, the fact it had to shut down during midday trading was one positive gleaned from the video shoot. Elsewhere it was business as usual with a mockery of the establishment game show *Who Wants To Be A Millionaire*.

This was paraphrased and featured as 'Who Wants To Be Filthy Fucking Rich', a reference to the fat cats of the stock exchange monopolies and corporations. The band were blasted as being 'anti-family' and 'pro-terrorist' by Gary Bauer, a Republican politician tied to various evangelical campaigns and organisations, who was cheekily quoted at the end of the video stating the band were called 'The Machine Rages On'.

Ironically the band were nominated for 'Best Rock Video' at the MTV Music Awards but Limp Bizkit beat them to the title with their 'Break Stuff' performance. Tim Commerford was not impressed, and when the polished white boy rappers responded by lip synching to the song on the MTV stage, Commerford climbed on top of the Bizkit stage set, almost bringing half of it down. He was subsequently arrested and slept overnight in a jail cell.

The emotional charge of 'Born Of A Broken Man' was one of the highlights of *The Battle Of Los Angeles*, a perfect amalgamation of highly personal lyrics and a luscious outpouring of emotion through the jagged musical textures. Some suggested it dealt with

Zack De La Rocha's father and the strained relationship the two.

"That song, it really has the most extreme dynamics that we've ever played," said Tom Morello. "It's got probably the mellowest Rage Against The Machine sentiment butted up against the heaviest riff ever recorded. All in the same song."

And Tim Commerford offered that it was the song that is "obviously the emotional side of Rage Against The Machine and Zack De La Rocha. It really is. It's just amazing how it just comes together from a very melodic kind of guitar part to this, just, huge monster of sound and back, and lyrically it's tear jerking. It's deep. It really is. I love it."

Though the album then dipped and swayed through the less remarkable ('Born As Ghosts') to the interesting but flawed ('Voice Of The Voiceless') and lyrically sure but musically predictable, it was at the climax of the record where Rage excelled again, cramming in two more tracks of vicious protest poetry.

'Ashes In The Fall' rated as one of the strongest tracks on the album. With a high pitched, torrid guitar beginning, the listener is unsure of just where this monster will grow, even when the almost basic rap infused brew begins. The song builds over the increasingly irate monologue before exploding in a cacophony of backing guitar, a true hardcore-meets-metal melding which supports the potent lyrics. One of Rage's most commanding and stirring numbers without question. On one internet forum, one user even went as far as to say, "When I turn this song up pretty loud with headphones on and implement certain buttons on the equalizer, I can achieve "audiorgasm" by listening to it. God, it feels good."

The closing track, 'War Within A Breath' was a more standard pattern of Rage filled venting, with a typical rising Morello guitar line, ably pinned by the thumping bass. It was the first time on the album Los Angeles had actually been referenced ("A risin' sun looming over Los Angeles") yet the song also name-checked the stealing of Mexican land once again and the inherent theme of world bankers and governors. The song and the album ends in a squealing mass of guitar torture, rounding off the 45-minute opus in a fashion which ultimately gives the listener the realisation they have just listened to something truly special. There was only one more thing to be done and that was start listening all over again.

You knew it was something special when Zack De La Rocha was happy with the product. "I think this is far and above the others in terms of its ability to fuse the elements of hip-hop, punk rock and urban Detroit rock music like MC5 and Iggy Pop," he beamed. "And there are moments where I think I've allowed more of my personal experiences to become part of the record."

So what of the title of the album? It was more than simply the members of Rage Against The Machine calling LA their home, in fact it made sense on many levels and instantly made reference to the likes of the LA riots and therefore, a revolution, beginning on their home streets. But the title also spoke for the rest of America as Tom Morello explained. "Los Angeles is sort of a microcosm of the rest of the world or the United States in general," he said. "It's a cultural mixing pot and everyone's sort of fighting for it. I just think that there's so many different problems and issues going on within Los Angeles itself. It does feel like a battle living in LA, period."

The contradictions to living in the 'City Of Angels' were radical and immediate for anyone who has visited the city, let alone lived there. Here was a place which enjoyed sunshine for up to 350 days of the year yet featured a permanent cloud of smog hovering over the city. There is a smorgasbord of colours and races co-habiting under the LA sky yet there is gang warfare and racial tension which always threatens to boil and blow beyond the city walls. It remains a place of the rich, ruling whites while police brutality is an every day occurrence for those living under the poverty line in the slums and ghettos of an otherwise affluent city.

"It is that complex cultural make-up of LA which makes a band like RATM possible," Tom would point out. "I think that Rage Against The Machine is a unique product of the city. It couldn't have happened anywhere else." And he added confrontationally, "There's a front that Hollywood puts out to the rest of the world as to what Los Angeles is, and that's only a very small slice of the real pie. *The Battle Of Los Angeles* is our version of events."

It may have been almost a decade on from the LA riots but much police corruption was still going by unnoticed and unchallenged in a bitter accompaniment to the release of the third

RATM record. There were several cases of corruption levelled against particular members of the Los Angeles Police Department (LAPD) at this time including reports of violence against a Mexican immigrant.

It was this persistent injustice which would stir action within the band on a local level. Brad Wilk for instance decided to create a program for local youngsters in the LA area. The Los Angeles Free Clinic is a non-profit organisation run by volunteers which exists to help young homeless people with food, shelter and medical attention.

The RATM drummer sought to enlist musicians in Los Angeles to help start a program which would teach kids how to play whichever instrument they wanted at no cost. "You'd think there'd be enough musicians in this area who have enough free time to go down there and help teach some of these kids," he mentioned to one drum magazine. "When I was growing up, music was a positive outlet that I think these kids really need."

And his views on his city of residence were mixed, much like his band mates. "Personally I have a love-hate relationship with LA," he told Ben Myers. "I have definitely been there long enough to let the things that would normally bother other people just wash over me. In the middle of all the phoney, back-stabbing entertainment music industry bullshit, there are actually lots of little pods of greatness to experience. Plus, it's such a cultural melting point. All that LA scenester shit is in your face if you want it to be, but that city has definitely had a large effect on every one of us in the band, both musically and politically."

The Battle of Los Angeles was released on November 2, 1999, entering the *Billboard* charts at Number 1 and proceeded to remain on the board for almost 40 weeks, peaking at #23 in the UK. *Kerrang!* were effervescent in their praise for the album, awarding it four K's. "Twelve songs of refined rock fury that blew the whistle on wrong-doers," *Kerrang!* wrote, "*The Battle of Los Angeles* is far more worldly than its title suggests. From Baghdad to DC, Hiroshima to Chiapas, this is the perfect collusion of Noam Chomsky analysis, Malcolm X radicalism and The Clash's sharp posturing."

Consistent with their ability to provoke and cause debate, RATM agreed to appear on the youth pop show *Total Request Live*, commonly known as *TRL*. They came in for heavy criticism for doing so but their reasons, as usual, served a dual purpose. Not only could they appear on a harmless pop show with their uncensored material, but they could provide a way for the uninitiated to perhaps take a different musical path in life than the type *TRL* would normally inspire. Besides, it came from the band's isolated upbringing and the understanding of what it was like to have stunted access to real culture.

Tom Morello explained, "I grew up in a place where there was no access to anything indie. None. One Musicland [store] within 40 miles. I never want to be élitist, and that's where a lot of kids see their music. We weren't going to skip the show because Britney Spears rather than Soundgarden may be on the day after us. The only concern for us is that the music and the politics are uncut. It's not like we are donning midriff outfits and sweaters in order to pander to the programmers or the audience."

And there was the ultimate reason of course, fit for not just the establishment but the kids themselves. Morello cracked, "*TRL* is where kids watch their rock. And we're going to do our best to terrify them."

Chapter Thirteen
Only The Good Die Young

From April 2000, Rage Against The Machine had been planning a special show, where they would perform by the Democratic National Convention. It seemed simple enough – make a stand against the ideology and unfairness of a two party system, play a free gig and get everyone rocking and then leave, having infiltrated the system one more time. However the reality of just one simple gig was far more convoluted simply because the security and planning around an event involving key political figures is always as stringent as it could possibly be. Picture the scenes in the vein of the series *24*, where wired up agents are constantly around the President and all the President's men. Though this series is entertaining enough, it is not merely fictional entertainment. On the contrary, these types of programmes are often given a seal of approval and accuracy from the top brass within the government. Therefore, those scenes you witness in such fictitious programmes are perhaps not far from the truth at all.

Rage had to gain permission to perform at the convention (which was held in corporate LA venue, the Staples Center) and it was initially denied with the band being told they would have to perform at a small venue several blocks away from the actual convention. Yet they were in luck when a US district court judge decreed this ruling too restrictive and allowed the band to go ahead in an area just opposite the DNC venue. The police reaction to a simple concert was extraordinary. They drew heavily on already strained public resources and made over 2000 officers available, all in riot gear. Additionally there were helicopters, police vehicles aplenty and mounted horses. Police sources admitted they were "gravely concerned because of security reasons."

But Rage were not about to let such an opportunity slip, especially when the crowd had grown to an estimated 50,000 people. De La Rocha made his statement from the stage, telling the crowd that their "democracy had been hijacked."

He also screamed, "We have a right to oppose these motherfuckers!" and made sure everyone looked in the direction of the DNC where Bill and Hillary Clinton were about to make their speeches.

Perhaps because of this, or maybe because it was going to happen anyway, scenes turned ugly. Writing for the *Independent Media Center*, Jennifer Bleyer reported on what happened next: "On Monday night, a peaceful, festive free show by Rage Against the Machine turned violent as cops finally got to show off all their months of anti-protest training at the Democratic National Convention. What began as a peaceful, festive march through downtown Los Angeles became violent tonight as police officers shot high-pressure water and pepper spray pellets at protesters, and later chased them down on horses while beating them with batons."

A standoff that lasted at least an hour ensued. While much of the crowd ambled off into the night, an estimated four thousand remained in the lot. A strange assortment of items found their way over the fence, including shoes, cardboard tubes, CDs, a handicapped parking sign, small bits of concrete and many plastic water bottles. In retaliation, the police opened fire at least five times on the protesters with pepper spray (which is shot in a capsule form that explodes on contact to emit a substance highly irritable to the eyes, nose and throat). In addition, they shot paint gun pellets, rubber bullets and water from a high-pressure hose through holes in the fence. A ranking police officer announced over a megaphone that the assembly had been declared unlawful, and that all those present were required to disperse or risk arrest. The protestors continued despite the stark opposition and did everything from chanting and climbing fences to waving black flags (to symbolise anarchy) and making a bonfire in the street. Unfortunately, despite all the melee this was barely noticed by the majority of reporters as they were safely ensconced in the centre covering the Clinton speeches.

Bleyer wrote, "After about an hour, the final straw of the standoff was drawn when about twenty police officers on horseback charged at the remaining few hundred protesters, many of whom were actually trying to leave the area when they were cornered. The horses stomped on people and chased them as the mounted cops swung their batons and yelled. At one point, four young Mexican-American men were thrown up against the fence by a cluster of horses while the mounted police officers beat them repeatedly with batons. The young men held their arms over their heads to protect themselves, and eventually were able to run from the attack."

It was typical of such events that by the time the people who had been inside the building with no knowledge of the rioting outside vacated it, there was barely any evidence of the previous few hours violence and unrest. Riot cops stood to attention as if only waiting for something to happen and just a few scraps of litter were still scattered on the ground. The blood had been cleared and the protestors escorted to the nearest jail cells.

Many witnesses who were not involved with the protestors later made complaints at unlawful and overly brutal police actions and the Union for American Civil Liberties decreed the melee as nothing less than "an orchestrated police riot." In response, the police claimed their actions were "clearly disciplined" and "outstanding". De La Rocha was indignant, asserting that the only rioting had emanated from the police, saying, "Those motherfuckers unloaded on this crowd. And I think it's ridiculous considering, you know, none of us had rubber bullets, none of us had M16s, none of us had billy clubs, none of us had face shields." RATM's documenting of the incident was captured for posterity on the *Live At The Grand Olympic Auditorium* DVD extras.

Musically Rage would continue their message with an interesting addition to their catalogue and one which was relatively unexpected. Everyone knew Rage had a broad combination of influences and any eclectic music fan could reference many of them, but RATM were about to pay true reverence to the originators of their rock meets rap style on their covers albums *Renegades*. The choices were somewhat unusual however. There was no Public Enemy, Clash, Led Zeppelin or

Black Sabbath – four bands which the RATM collective had often name-checked, especially Tom Morello. Perhaps the band viewed these as too obvious (though they could have chosen lesser known tracks). Instead, it was to the kinds of groups many young fans may have only read about, such as MC5, Iggy & The Stooges in terms of the rock genre, oddities such as Devo, and basic hip-hop representation in the form of EPMD and Eric B & Rakim. Equally intriguing was the fact that within the album inlay there was no direct credit given to the original song writers, no recommendation to go check out the back catalogue of any artists you may have been intrigued by. It was overall a fairly low key release which, as was now expected with Rage, seemed somewhat less appealing than it eventually revealed itself to be. Still, armed with a knowledge of the original tracks and then RATM's subsequent dismantling and re-energising their adaptations took on a whole new level; and perhaps in not naming the original renegades, Rage were expecting listeners to do their homework or maybe even already be aware of the songs being covered.

The rap original of Eric B & Rakim's 'Microphone Fiend' was one of the most obvious updates on the rap blueprint. Hard hitting and heavy drums gave an instant smack to proceedings with the fluid Commerford bass line accompanying perfectly. Despite the song being a relatively faithful recreation of the hip-hop style of the original, there was another obvious addition on the verse with the funky clapping of guitar strings before the chorus slammed in with major guitar backing. The original had no such luxury, skipping along at a snail's pace with minimal emphasis on a chorus. The principal difference between rock and rap was thus illuminated, but Rage cleverly brought the two disparate genres together, showing if anything just how they truly had fired up the sometimes flat rap genre with the vibrant sprinkling of real guitar, bass and drums – no syncopated rhythms here.

Such was Morello's creative force that he could add his own style to virtually any existing song, as on the opener where he lent a riff to a song which originally contained none. Though De La Rocha was clearly paying homage and giving faithful recreation as far as the basic rap went, there was no doubting he indulged the song with an added depth of spitting personality, but then this guy

153

could make a Michael Bolton song sound interesting.

Up next was the closest thing to an original on the *Renegades* album, with Rage merging a classic by funksters Zapp (the gorgeously named 'More Bounce To The Ounce') with their own stylee, creating an original thriving dance floor classic 'Pistol Grip Pump'. The literal bouncing heartbeat combination of bass, drum and guitar resonated long after the song finished and was the kind of bulging rhythm which would become lodged in the brain for many hours. In fact, after the first spin of the *Renegades* album, this was likely to be the one outstanding memory.

'Kick Out The Jams' is one of the best known punk rock anthems of all-time and a lengthy list of artists have covered it in the 40 years since it was first recorded by Detroit's MC5. In order for a band to cover the song in modern times, they needed to alter the song to make it stand out from the hundreds of other, straightforward cover versions in existence. Rage did just that. The first thing you noticed is how slow the song is, almost lounge-like in its direction, losing about half the beat and featuring Zack De La Rocha in perhaps his first real bout of sustained singing. As he ably demonstrated, his voice was multi-levelled and adaptable. At first the low slung intimacy of this version was a disappointment and didn't sound like MC5 *or* Rage Against The Machine (the live version included on the album is actually faster paced and more in line with the original). But the slow creeping funk gradually wormed its way in and ultimately listeners were left admiring Rage for taking such a unique approach to a well-worn classic. There was even time for a more customary Tom Morello solo full of unusual textures.

Not only was MC5 co-founder Wayne Kramer impressed with the adaptation, he even commented on Rage's political approach and its benefits. "The stuff that Rage Against The Machine is talking about is essentially what the MC5 were talking about," he commented to the *Chicago Tribune*, "that all liberals and revolutionaries have talked about in this country going back to Thomas Paine. And it's not glamorous or sexy or exciting. We're talking about justice, education, health care and jobs – the fundamental building blocks of civilisation."

Up next was the riff of the album (and centrepiece) of the

record. While covering 'Renegades Of Funk', Rage catapulted a tremendous funky riff with a deep rounded undertone, propping up the explosive word play perfectly. The song name-checked the likes of Dr Martin Luther King, Malcolm X and the aforementioned Tom (Thomas) Paine, an English revolutionary, combining this recognition of radical historical figures with the call for the new coming of a revolution – beginning with ordinary people.

This was the perfect song for Rage to tackle, consisting of the ultimate lyrics on revolution and the perfect backing jam, pumped up to the max. Perhaps the most impressive lyrical display on the album came from this song, De La Rocha rapping at the speed of light, so fast in fact that you can barely even follow the words in time, even with a lyric sheet. The original version by Afrika Bambaataa would disappoint those who happened upon it due to Rage's cover version. Consisting of a persistent, dull thumping drum beat, reminiscent of the early Eighties rap beats and barely grooving vocal lines which are intermittent at best, the song sounds more like a bad accompaniment to an Eighties soundtrack as opposed to a revolutionary call to arms. Rage just showed once again how broad their talents were and just how they could turn an old recording into something magnificent.

Call it pop, synth, new wave, post-punk or just some quirky shit – the quintet known as Devo are an outfit regularly name-checked by heaps of alternative thinking musicians. Their mostly upbeat material was catchy yet equally too unusual to ever be fully mainstream. Of all the tracks for RATM to cover, the most unlikely might seem to be 'Beautiful World' yet it's fair to say the band made it their own and brought an unlikely emotional quality to proceedings, placed beautifully between the mighty funk slab of 'Renegades…' and the following hip-hop brawl of 'I'm Housin'. Damn, this track almost stole the show with a whispered cusp of emotion drawing breath only to lament the melancholy lyrics. These, when read soberly on a page seemed innocuous and virtually meaningless but when enunciated crisply and shakily heartfelt by De La Rocha, the song took new life, breathing a lovelorn quality into proceedings.

The EPMD original of 'I'm Housin' is straight up hip-hop with a low slung vibe, reminiscent of Tone Loc. There was no thumping guitar or separation for the 'chorus' chant of "Cos I'm Housin'", that was something Rage added. Still, De La Rocha showed his capable rap nous and replicated the verses with aplomb. With the combined guitar background noises and the hushed word play, the song took on a spooky edge, before erupting into the chorus once again, showing that even the most ordinary original could be fired up with the right gathering of capable musicians.

Minor Threat's 'In My Eyes' was tackled next. The original was typical of the Ian Mackaye troupe, dripping in Eighties hardcore angst: fast, furious and tinny. Rage simply lent the original a new buoyancy and a dextrous Morello performance. The song gave all the band members license to tap into their furious punk origins via one of the greatest bands to ever emerge from hardcore.

Zack showed he still had the fury and capability to draw upon his early influences and expound them frantically on CD, dropping the mighty lyrics which seemed to sum up RATM with a clairvoyant touch: *"You tell me that I make no difference, at least I'm fuckin' trying/What the fuck have you done?"*

In deference to another hip-hop outfit, it seemed fitting to cover a song by famed tokers Cypress Hill. They went with 'How I Could Just Kill A Man', a track from the band's self-titled debut album but in truth it was the only track Rage really failed to ignite with their own style, the expected guitar funk sounding too contrived and the lack of a nasally front man (a la Cypress chief vocalist B-Real) meant the material sounded void of direction and just another rap rock number, blending in alongside other ordinary tracks of the time. Both RATM and Cypress Hill were better than this. In fact, the latter would gradually up the heaviness in their repertoire as their career progressed, eventually peaking with a full on rock set in the 'Bones' section of their fifth album, the double *Skull & Bones* set.

The combination of the original spirit for 'How I Could Just Kill A Man' and the added Rage bite was evident, and made more sense, on the live version included at the end of the *Renegades* album, where Cypress' B-Real and Sen Dog duet with Rage.

After the inclusion of the Springsteen cover 'The Ghost Of Tom Joad' (on an album for the first time), it was onto the Stooges cover, 'Down On The Street'. Again, lots of bands paid lip service to the great Iggy Pop with a variation of bog standard and sometimes decent cover versions, but this particular track was one of the lesser known songs from the Stooges' second album, *Fun House*. At the time, 1970, this album went down like a lead balloon but was subsequently heralded as being influential for a whole raft of hardcore, punk and alternative musicians There were a whole host of Stooges tracks which might have been better suited to Rage but they clearly took pride in choosing the less predictable route, and in the process merely underlined how unique their own material was.

Perhaps one of their more self-explanatory choices was the cover of the Rolling Stones' 'Street Fighting Man' though reading into the lyrics their methodology became clearer. "Hey! Think the time is right for a palace revolution," swaggers Mick Jagger, "But where I live the game to play is compromise solution …" Yes this was more like it! True Rage propaganda and the band successfully breathed new life into a well worn rock standard, giving it greater urgency and effervescence.

When *Renegades* worked, it highlighted the wealth of talent at Rage's disposal and managed to show all bases of their innovative sound, whilst simultaneously showing the beauty in the original songs – not an easy thing to do. On the odd occasions where it didn't quite pay off, well it was still darn good. The album wouldn't have been complete without a paean to the protest folk blues of Bob Dylan and it came in the shape of 'Maggie's Farm', from 1965. Here was one of the better conversions from primitive guitar and vocal to full on rock behemoth tactics. The sentiments echoed Rage's protest ethic, socialist roots and De La Rocha delivered another faultless interpretation on yet another different style of music.

The album was also notable as being produced chiefly by Rick Rubin (with RATM in assistance and Brendan O'Brien popping up for 'The Ghost Of Tom Joad'). This rap rock mogul who had overseen the careers of the likes of both Slayer and the Beastie Boys was a perfect match for Rage Against The Machine, though it was interesting to note that his usual style of pitching each song up against the next with barely a pause in the transition was lacking on *Renegades*. Each song was given time to breathe. With such an in depth, complex array of songs this was probably a wise move. The *Renegades* album would not be released until the end of 2000, but by this time Rage Against The Machine had shocked their fans … by disbanding.

Fans around the world pored over the statement issued by Zack De La Rocha to explain the shock news that Rage Against The Machine had split up. In it, he explained the reasons for the break up and also pointed out that Morello, Wilk and Commerford would stay together in their next band.

"I feel that it is now necessary to leave Rage because our decision-making process has completely failed," Zack said in his October 18 statement. "It is no longer meeting the aspirations of all four of us collectively as a band, and from my perspective, has undermined our artistic and political ideal."

What had actually been RATM's last show featured a rousing speech from the singer, before the band launched into 'Killing In The Name'. Here he laid out the diatribe against the events following the band's set outside the DNC. He added, "All we had was our fists, our voices, our microphones, our guitars, our drums, our timbales and what-not. And any time we get beaten in the streets for protesting, we take it to the court system, but the court system don't wanna hear it. Look what happened to Amadou Diallo in New York. They shot that brother 41 times and let all four officers go. It's time for a new type of action in this country."

The man De La Rocha referred to was a 23-year-old Guinean immigrant who was approached because he allegedly matched the description of a serial rapist in the area. Though the rapist had not struck for nine months, police approached the 'suspect' with force, and believing he took out a gun (it was actually a wallet) fired at him, as De La Rocha said, 41 times – 19 of which actually hit Diallo. The four officers in question were all tried before a jury but they were all found not guilty of any wrongdoing. Many protestors spoke out against the unjust case, including actress Susan Sarandon and the Reverend Jesse Jackson – this was a case, which invoked reaction from all walks of life. Diallo was a simple street peddler, barely making a living and had no previous convictions or any connection whatsoever to any wrongdoing. It was mistaken identity but 41 bullets wouldn't have been necessary to quell a small army, much less a harmless man standing motionless on the steps of a building. Diallo would not even have known he was being fired at by police officers as all four were dressed in plain clothes at the time.

There were many other non-famous protestors and in the following weeks varying protests resulted in 1700 arrests. Diallo's parents won a subsequent lawsuit, to the tune of $3,000,000 for the racial profiling, gross negligence and wrongful death of their son. It begged the question, if the officers were not at fault, why would the Diallos receive a payout for all the reasons the officers were sent to trial in the first place?

With such cases in mind, it was clear De La Rocha felt there was nothing further he could do within the boundaries of Rage Against The Machine. And for all their political angst and subversive rhetoric, it seemed one of the greatest bands of the last few decades were going to succumb to that old chestnut: creative differences. Tom Morello wanted to continue to push the boundaries and take Rage to a new level, furthering their political stance and making bigger and bolder statements. De La Rocha felt they should retreat into relative obscurity and embrace their hardcore, independent roots.

Strangely, he seemed to be against the release of the *Renegades* album, despite the fact he had recorded it. According to Ben Myers in *American Heretics: Rebel Voices In Music*, Zack "vehemently opposed" the *Renegades* album release, "on the grounds that the band were conforming to standard record company ways of milking a cash cow. His band-mates reacted by hiring new management for themselves and pushing on with the release anyway."

There were still musical reasons behind the split, as Zack illuminated to *Spin* magazine. "Every time we entered a studio, this arm wrestling match would start between what I heard, which was more of an Afrika Bambaataa meets Sonic Youth type of thing, and what Tom heard, which was Jimmy Page and Tony Iommi," he sighed. "It rarely extended past those boundaries and that slow evolution was one of the reasons I became so exhausted. Toward the end it was clear that there were no musical risks being taken. You could basically tell what a Rage record was going to sound like before you even heard it."

The band's final two shows, recorded on September 12 and 13 at the Grand Olympic Auditorium in Los Angeles (a fitting city for the story to end), were captured and released for posterity as a live album, the unimaginatively titled *Live At The Grand Olympic Auditorium*, though this would not come out for another three years.

Even as an inactive band, Rage managed to upset the status quo of popular music. After the events of September 11, 2001, the Clear Channel Corporation decided to create a list of songs with "questionable lyrics". It was, of course, highly necessary to focus on the mere words of rock bands as opposed to bringing to justice those responsible for the domestic attacks. The Clear Channel list featured one record-breaking group – Rage Against The Machine – who held the distinction of every single one of their songs appearing on the list.

"There's only been a few times in my history as a musician and an activist where I've ever felt 'the Man' push back," quipped Tom Morello. "One of them was the immediate aftermath of 9/11. Clear Channel banned all Rage Against The Machine songs from all their radio stations. They faxed this memorandum to all the stations that listed specific songs that could not be played, including John Lennon's 'Imagine' and the Gap Band's 'You Dropped A Bomb On Me'. The only artist whose entire catalogue was singled out was Rage Against The Machine."

There was also the spat with the organisation that called itself Rock For Life. They levelled accusations at Rage Against The Machine – and Tom Morello especially – in with one particular press release. He was cited as a "baby killer" and accused of hating Christians and making music which was nothing more than "hateful propaganda".

Luckily Tom Morello found the funny side, telling an Australian radio station, "I really didn't know anything about the organisation before that, it's hard to believe whether that press release is ignorance or whether that it is just ingenious. You know, because they describe Rage Against The Machine as supporting 'hate-crimes' which couldn't be anything further from the truth. And while we absolutely have played benefit concerts, I think in '93, for 'Rock For Choice' which stands up for women's rights for abortion rights ... you know, that's something which we've absolutely done and continue to stand up for – sexual discrimination of any kind ... Jeez!"

Indignantly he continued, "Rock For Life didn't seem to have any interest in starting any sort of dialogue with the band. Apart from the ten out of eleven inaccuracies in their press release, they didn't do much back checking before they put it out, so we could have set them straight. I mean I'd be delighted to debate any topic with any of those fools from that organisation any day of the week!"

Rock For Life is part of the American Life League, a Christian organisation who opposes abortion. RFL is designed to bring a voice to their causes through bands who share the same 'pro-life' views. "Young people are being deceived and manipulated by the music industry!" their official website claims. "Many of today's popular artists speak out for abortion rights and raise money for pro-abortion causes. They are feeding our youth with the lie that abortion is not only an answer to their problems, but a right they must fight to protect."

A show that RATM had played in Mexico City in 1999 was afforded a posthumous release on video and DVD. The show itself is powerful in sections, yet in others lacks the spark of many of the best Rage performances. It is almost as if the notion of playing in Mexico City for the first time has Zack so coiled and passionate he can barely sing all the words to every song for the fury wound up inside him. Yet it's not just the singer who isn't at full mast, the band was occasionally cumbersome, slowing down the impact of 'Know Your Enemy' in particular by altering the tempo. And the edit often ruins the impact of certain segments by slowing down the picture in the wrong areas, cheapening the ferocity of the songs – it looks more like *Top Of The Pops* than a revolutionary concert.

Still, the fervent crowd maintain the energy levels and mix their fury with respect for certain parts or full songs which are less about rocking out and more concerned with the lyrics. When the hush of 'Zapata's Blood' blows across the auditorium, the crowd savour every line and even on the more personal 'Born Of A Broken Man' the crowd stands silent at the quieter section as in respect of the intimacy of the lyrics. At the end of 'Freedom', De La Rocha drops to his knees, completely spent, barely able to pick himself up again, then just before the credits roll Zack and Tom leave the stage arms round each other like life-long friends.

Tickets had been cheap (unlike most shows in the area) and all proceeds went to the victims of a recent flood in southern Mexico. "About two days before the show, we received a letter from Subcommandante Marcos," Morello explained, "asking us to give the money not to the communities where his Zapatista fighters are, but rather to the flood victims from the recent flood there, we were happy to do it." Interspersed within the music on the DVD are clips of spoken word and flashing images which give background to the Mexican causes De La Rocha involves himself with.

For Rage fans it was the first time they could witness Subcommandante Marcos as there was an interview with him on the DVD of the Mexico City show. Though dressed in army fatigues and carrying weaponry whilst hidden by a balaclava, Marcos comes across as humanitarian and extremely intelligent. His eyes portray a sadness and empathy yet also suggest he is not a man to be messed with. Naturally he is chiefly concerned with the Zapatistas, yet much of what he says can be applied to the world at large and other sections of society which are repressed. Of all the sections of the DVD, his interview is perhaps the most important.

RATM's gig was not without its difficulties; as so often the case, it was an achievement just for them to make it on stage. At the time the band were due to play the show, there had been student strikes going on in the city and the combination of this and criticism from 'foreigners' such as RATM who were criticising the Mexican government did not sit well with the authorities. The reason the resulting DVD was called *The Battle Of Mexico City* was due to the fact that before the band were due to go onstage a riot started outside the venue due to the massive number of people who couldn't fit into the venue and didn't hold a ticket. Estimates were made that there were approximately 7,000 inside the venue and a further 3,000 who couldn't get in and thus began to try and break barricades down to storm the venue. Riot police were called and fired tear gas to disperse the crowd.

"There was also a huge student strike going on over there at the moment and the Mexican government doesn't tolerate criticism from Mexican citizens let alone foreign nationals," Tom Morello explained. "So there was a great deal of controversy surrounding the show but in the end it went off pretty great and we were able to raise money for those flood victims who were in need, so it was a pretty damn rocking show!"

Morello was referring to the strike against UNAM in Mexico City, Mexico's largest public university with 270,000 students – incidentally a university which Marcos attended. The Mexican constitution promises a free education to Mexican citizens. UNAM announced in 1999 that tuition would rise from 2 cents to $150 a year. This is a huge amount for most Mexican people, where the minimum wage is less than $4 a day. One in two Mexicans live below the official poverty line and a quarter of the population live in extreme poverty. Even with virtually free tuition, many young Mexicans are effectively denied access to UNAM because they can't pay for the cost of books, transportation and other expenses. The students demonstrated en masse in the city centre and eventually barricaded themselves in the university raising red and black banners to declare a strike.

But this was not about to stop the band protesting at the injustices of the poverty stricken communities. "It is what it is, I can't help it. I just gotta feel it, what I see," De La Rocha said. "Every time I come back from there I learn. I just try to channel it, all that fear. I remember one time we were sleeping in this little school house, me and a lot of the students I helped to organise to get down there. We were in this schoolhouse and the army was trying to run weapons through the village at night and the dogs were barking, we were fucking terrified. And I thought if I had to experience this every day that would be life in hell. So I just come back here and try to let people know there's people out there that don't even have what you have and [are] trying to get something to survive."

Also on the DVD, De Le Rocha had a chance to interview

Noam Chomsky, an experience he was clearly grateful for, seemingly in awe of the legendary political commentator. In fact, the singer looked up to Chomsky with the same eyes of adulation and respect his millions of fans around the world offered him.

As Zack De La Rocha made his way to the confines of a low key existence away from the demands of the rock scene and the persistent pressure on his personal life, the remaining members of Rage Against The Machine had a choice to make. Should they continue without him? It wasn't ever really up for debate as to whether they would continue making music together. This instrumental triumvirate was well versed, tight and focused – not to mention hailing the respect and admiration of millions around the world. The only question was whether to continue as Rage Against The Machine, with a replacement for De La Rocha, or to start an entirely new band.

Though the rumours of a new Rage singer were rife, the band would settle on the latter option. The overwhelming favourite to take over at the helm of Rage was Cypress Hill's B-Real. However, there were also rumours of the more appealing choice of Rey Oropeza from rap-core legends Downset (a superb band – the exceedingly talented Oropeza could have aptly handled the De La Rocha style). Frankly it seemed a little odd that B-Real was even mooted as front man for Rage Against The Machine. For one, his somnambulant vocal style, though suitably bubbly where needed, was nowhere near potent enough for the Rage material. Could anyone honestly imagine him fronting the likes of 'Killing In The Name'? No, Rage would have been reduced to a carnival act, carrying on like lounge-core versions of their own selves.

Clearly, Morello and his cohorts realised this fairly early on, and the rumours certainly seemed to come from beyond the band's control. They were about to go for something drastic, but it wasn't anything which could have been predicted. They were going to start a new band with a completely different style of singer. It was going to be called Audioslave and would feature one of the greatest modern vocalists in the world of rock music. They had just bagged a singer called Christopher John Boyle. People knew him better as Chris Cornell.

Chapter Fourteen
Slaves To The Power

Chris Cornell was born on July 20, 1964 and grew up in Seattle. His family was stable yet Cornell was prone to a feeling of isolation that was only exacerbated by his tendency to lock himself away alone listening to music and learning how to play The Beatles songs on guitar and drums. When he was twenty, however, he finally found a viable outlet for his emotions when he formed Soundgarden (named after a Seattle sculpture), originally playing drums as well as singing.

Though the careers of Cornell and his future Rage Against The Machine band mates were vastly different, they shared two things in common, one of which was they both knew what mass success from nowhere felt like. The other was more subliminal but is interesting to note in hindsight. Soundgarden guitarist Kim Thayil became one of the greatest musicians of his generation, and though he would eventually be placed as 100th best guitarist of all-time by *Rolling Stone* magazine was still distinctly underrated. He is not only a superb guitar player, but an innovative songwriter to boot. He is of Indian descent, both his parents coming to America from the Indian state of Kerala. Another of the founding members was bass player Hiro Yamamoto who, though born in Seattle, was of Japanese descent.

It was no deliberate move on the band's part, of course. They didn't plan to concoct a mixed race group to garner attention and in fact it didn't even work out that way. The band were never less than respected due to their music and most didn't seem to even notice the band was of mixed race. Yet, this in itself was an achievement in the colour driven separatism of the time and the wariness with which the white establishment approached ethnic newcomers. It was simply unusual to see a band who looked so different to the accepted norms of hard rock. Inadvertently then, Soundgarden helped to break down the doors of prejudice within the music industry.

Yamamoto would leave the band after 1989's *Louder Than Love*, an album which began to make waves for the band and featured a host of future live favourites from 'Hands All Over' to 'Loud Love'. The album would soon be eclipsed by the band's follow-up but, much like their very early material (*Screaming Life* and *Fopp* EPs followed by the *Ultramega OK* album) it was diverse, exciting and highly recommended. It was also the first time the music world was introduced to the truly awesome larynx of Chris Cornell, who could reach ludicrously high notes without straining or losing any power.

Still, when Soundgarden released the mighty *Badmotorfinger*, album they went from background staples of the Seattle scene to one of the leaders. Though clearly overshadowed in terms of popularity by both Nirvana and Pearl Jam, Soundgarden were easily the most wide-ranging artists of all the grunge icons of the Nineties. Their material encompassed everything from psychedelia and flower pop to heavy metal and hardcore. Many bands are cited as innovative or unmistakeable but this was never truer than with Soundgarden who were immediately recognisable from both Thayil's landmark licks and Cornell's throaty, heartfelt vocal swagger. This band knew their brilliance but carried it with remarkable understatement – throwing out emotional classics and hard rock greats as if they were doing a school project.

The band were on a major label (A&M) yet managed to retain their integrity and creative flow, releasing a stunning set of songs. Dripping with classics, *Badmotorfinger* was an hour of magnificent musicianship and memorable, timeless melodies, topped off with the broad ranging, powerful vocals of Cornell. He hit new heights with the likes of 'Jesus Christ Pose', recording a range few vocalists in the world could match. The band were on fire throughout the entire album, whether on the singles 'Outshined' and 'Rusty Cage' or the less immediate but no less brilliant album-only tracks, in particular 'Room A Thousand Years Wide', 'Mind Riot' and 'Somewhere'.

Though the band came to be revered, and were already making head waves at the time of *Badmotorfinger*, there were few who truly understood the band – diversity was a dirty word in the caverns of early Nineties rock music. "I love Soundgarden 'cos every time they release an album I get a new Sabbath record," one musician stated. Chris Cornell was told this misinformed statement and responded to *Raw Power*, "Whoever said that doesn't know what they're talking about." (That would be Mötley Crüe's Nikki Sixx.)

The same year, Cornell joined up with his friends in Pearl Jam (and with 'Garden drummer Matt Cameron) to create a spellbinding side project known as Temple Of The Dog. Less severe than Soundgarden, they were emotional and understated and even hinted at a soft rock tendency with certain tracks – pre-empting Cornell's future direction.

Soundgarden's biggest selling album came in 1994 when they released *Superunknown*, which went on to top numerous charts around the world and sell several million copies. Many of the singles indicated this was a completely different band to the one that had recorded *Badmotorfinger* – more streamlined and verging on mainstream. Inevitably the most popular songs were those which were essentially power ballads – 'Fell On Black Days', 'The Day I Tried To Live' and a song for which Soundgarden would from then on be most associated – 'Black Hole Sun'. Though these were decent songs, they weren't a patch on their antecedent album. Equally the release of such singles detracted from the fact there were still a few heavier tracks in the bleachers – notably the title track and 'Fresh Tendrils'. Still, 'Spoonman' and 'My Wave', which were also singles, were respectable straightforward, catchy rock numbers.

Yet Soundgarden were morphing away from their past, and even their multitude of new fans were left somewhat unimpressed with the final album from the band. *Down On The Upside* was an uninspired title and an even less inspiring set of songs in general, though there were occasional rays of sunshine with the emotive 'Blow Up The Outside World' (arguably one of their best songs) and the passable 'Pretty Noose'.

The group disbanded on April 9, 1997, leaving behind a small yet highly influential and occasionally extraordinary body of work.

Cornell used his free time to begin a solo career but his resulting album, *Euphoria Morning*, was only sporadically entertaining and failed to ignite his legion of fans. He wouldn't truly hit the heights of fame experienced at the peak of Soundgarden's zenith until he found the ex-members of Rage Against The Machine, a band he had the utmost respect for.

Cornell had been an innovator in the modern world of alternative music and so, in many ways, although seemingly ill-fitting at first, was actually perfectly aligned with the trend setting antics of Morello and Co. Still, it was a brave choice. *Euphoria Morning* was an understated, melancholy set of songs, very much at odds with even the lighter side of Soundgarden. It almost seemed as if he had fallen out of love with the hard rock side of things. Clearly, in many interviews the singer gave, he often stated it was nice not to have to "shout" anymore when performing. Given the likes of the early Soundgarden material, so high and mighty, it was no wonder he wanted to gradually streamline his vocal performance. Still, it was difficult to reconcile the might and frantic rap attack of RATM with the now laid-back crooning of Cornell.

It was just one of many innovations Tom Morello can perhaps take credit for. To be able to envisage Chris Cornell taking on the elaborate material he and his band mates were capable of creating was visionary to say the least. Still, he wasn't alone in his proclamation that Cornell would make a great singer for their new group. On the contrary, he was backed by Commerford, Wilk and new friend Rick Rubin.

The latter seemed to be exercising his familiar role of guardian angel to certain bands he works with. Rubin has two forms as producer. On one hand, he can simply do the production job with little further interaction, if the band either does not want or need his extra input. Or he can take a shine to a band so much that he seeks to be integrated into the line-up as virtual fifth member, offering personal and professional advice, further to his musical counsel. Such involvement from an 'outsider' can have adverse effects and Rubin was treading a fine line with his new charges.

Millions of Metallica fans (as well as interested voyeurs) around the world have laughed, cried or scoffed at their *Some Kind Of*

Monster movie, where the band tries to get to grips with the recording of their *St. Anger* album. The band faces singer James Hetfield's rehabilitation, a complete breakdown in communication and a surprising lack of musical chemistry. All this as well as having to find and integrate a new bass player. It is immediately clear that, for a band who have been together for twenty years, they seem painfully unable to communicate with any clarity, and as the band admit, they don't know each other very well at all. This understanding creates a cringeworthy aspect to the film, it feels embarrassing in parts and is bitter to watch. Band members, especially Hetfield and drummer Lars Ulrich, are often in abrupt discussions which at one stage culminates in a huge verbal unloading between the two Metallica leaders.

The ongoing interaction of group therapist and performance coach Phil Towle was a core part of the film – he'd been brought in to help smooth over the cracks in the band's relationships. However, as the movie draws to a close, the band sack the coach. Similarly, here is where Rick Rubin's involvement with the new band was potentially fraught with risk. As the ex-RATM trio convened with Chris Cornell, Rick Rubin suggested they meet with Phil Towle for some much needed group therapy.

De La Rocha was never a negative influence, but it was the unusual chemistry between him and Morello which had brought the creative difficulties – as well as the artistic highs. Given they were the two chiefly responsible for merging music and lyrics together, they were the main thrust of the band's muse.

So, with De La Rocha out of the picture, it seemed extraneous to appoint someone to help with the creative flow and personal trials within the group. At a push you could perhaps argue for the need to banish all previous demons and begin anew. After all, the band now had to transfer all their emotional baggage into a new scenario with a new singer and they could well adversely influence proceedings before they even really began. Equally, unlike Metallica, Rage Against The Machine had the mantle of political activists to contend with and this undoubtedly affected their personal relationships with each other.

"It kind of sucks," Tim Commerford told *Raygun* magazine, "because somehow the music has almost taken a back seat to the politics of the band. Me personally? I'm totally into issues, but at the same time it's hard for me, because I started playing bass because I wanted to play music, not because I wanted to be a politician. And it's really difficult because now every time I do an interview, it's always a political thing and I feel like it's really hard for me to say something that's potent politically, because I've got a couple of guys in my band who are *sooooo* into politics. Like, what else can I say that Tom hasn't already covered in his ten years of political science and studies? I could read a book a day for the rest of my life and still probably not know as much as Tom knows about politics."

He also gave further insight into his private life when he expanded, "I think to a certain extent it's harder to be personal than it is to be political. It really is. It's like, you can get the knowledge to be political, and learn, and then you're political. You understand it and now you're a political person, but to be personal – sometimes it takes tragedy in your life in order to become somebody who understands things on a personal level, and that's kind of the story of my life ... my life up until I was like, 20 years old is kind of a blur."

After the intervention of both Rubin then Towle, Commerford referred to the former as "the angel at the crossroads because if it wasn't for him I wouldn't be here today." We will probably never know exactly what went on behind closed doors, but clearly there were issues that needed to be resolved and Rubin was savvy enough to spot it and address them before moving on to his more expected role as producer. The introduction of Phil Towle could have been more of a hindrance than help yet it seemed to pay off.

The meetings with Towle were used to shed the skin of the past and move on to concentrate on the new relationship the band were going to have with a singer. If there were any fears on how the chemistry would develop, they were soon allayed when the band entered a room to jam with Cornell.

"He stepped to the microphone and sang the song and I couldn't believe it," Morello beamed. "It didn't just sound good. It didn't sound great. It sounded transcendent. And when there is an irreplaceable chemistry from the first moment, you can't deny it."

It was already something the band members agreed on but the

subject had to be broached. How exactly did they want to sound? Would it be a combination of Rage Against The Machine and Soundgarden, or would it just be one of the two? Perhaps it would be neither. Or maybe, just maybe, these musicians were talented enough to take their smorgasbord of influences – as well as their former careers – and combine it in one huge melting pot of originality. That is indeed what happened, and everyone agreed they did not want to replicate anything which had come in their past. It was all to be naturally developed with a reliance on their talents to turn the music into a coherent collaboration.

The band averaged more than a song a day for their first few weeks together, ultimately creating twenty-one unique sound frames. The moniker for their new alliance was Audioslave, a name conjured up by Chris Cornell. There are conflicting reports that the band were originally going to be called Civilian until they found another band had the name, but Tom Morello disputes the notion, claiming the only name the band ever had was Audioslave.

Strangely, for such a seemingly unusual name, it came to light that an unsigned band in Liverpool were already using it. Reports suggested they were paid a sizeable fee by Morello and Co. so that both bands could continue using the name. Stranger still was the widespread criticism of the name, with magazines from *Spin* to *Pitchfork Media* slamming the choice of moniker, calling it everything from "one of the dumbest names in rock history" to "most asinine band name of the year".

Still, interest was immense in just how the former members of two of the biggest modern rock bands would sound when welded together. In the world of corporate rock it didn't even matter. It seemed they knew this band would sell in their droves. As such, Audioslave were approached by Ozzfest, to appear at the seventh version of the festival, despite not having any confirmed material or, at that time, even a confirmed name. Then, suddenly it seemed, all the in-house coaching and therapy might not have worked – at least that's how it seemed at first – when it was rumoured the band had broken up before they could even record and release their first album. Reports of Chris Cornell leaving the group in March 2002 were apparently confirmed by management representatives.

Though there was no explanation given, it soon emerged that

Cornell had a problem with the band being run by two different managers. He had Guerinot while the ex-RATM alliance was managed by Peter Mensch of Q Prime (one half of Metallica's management team). In the end, the new band took on a new management team known as The Firm. There were also wrangles between the two record companies understandably battling it out to release the first Audioslave album, but both Epic and Interscope settled on a compromise whereby they would release albums alternately.

By May 2002, the band had thirteen demo tracks but before they could be refined and polished, somehow they were leaked and quickly spread across the multitude of peer-to-peer file sharing networks across the internet. The band were upset because these were clearly not finished and it was not the way they wanted everyone to hear their new alliance. Some songs were just not finished; others were mere skeletons of their eventual form with guitar solos or lyrics completely different to the finished product.

Still it wouldn't be long before the final finished tracks were available. The album was preceded by single, 'Cochise'. It was obvious just how different this band was to its predecessors, though the unmistakable vocals of Chris Cornell inevitably hinted at latterday Soundgarden. The regular, and lazy, comparisons of this kind of band to the likes of Led Zeppelin and Black Sabbath inevitably rained down upon the new material. Yet, in truth, their direction had little in common with Sabbath and a bare similarity to Led Zeppelin. The latter were an emotional band who could ably rock out at 100 miles an hour or plaintively strum their melancholy blues, which upon first glance would be a perfect summation of Audioslave.

Yet it was a redundant comparison because, though Led Zeppelin were the innovators and firmly established classic artists, Audioslave had more at their disposal. They could write memorable songs as well as update the Morello squeaks and squawks which somehow carried a tune. Chris Cornell was no Robert Plant but then he had more than enough talent of his own and his voice was completely different.

Rick Rubin thought the band, at their best, could attain the level of "Yardbirds meets Zeppelin" yet this was an aim which could perhaps never be reached. The persistent suggestion that this was a band who were rocking like 1970 all over again was flawed. Given Morello's modern and innovative style, there was little other than the fact here was a band using guitar, bass and drums, to compare them with rock groups of the Seventies. Debut album *Audioslave* was a modern *sounding* record, full of adept rocking moments and soulful plaintive turns, more in line with the era of grunge than anything else. Unless this band came out wearing stack heels, huge wigs and playing like Slade were all the rage, the assertion of Audioslave being a Seventies throwback was crass and just plain wrong.

Furthermore, it was always other people who talked of these supposed influences and convergence of sounds, never the band members themselves. They were simply on their own trip, occasionally making obvious hard rock or even soft rock references but almost exclusively doing their own thing which morphed and developed as they went along. There was no master plan; they were just naturally creating their art. And it sounded good. The debut album was a varied exorcism of a zillion different factors, and altogether *Audioslave* sounded like no one else. This uniqueness would be the biggest selling point of the record, as opposed to the novelty factor that there was some sort of super group in our midst.

'Cochise' was a formidable opening track, though somewhat at odds with the less aggressive material elsewhere on the record. Slowly coming in to a typically buoyant Morello riff, this was just the track to introduce Audioslave to the masses and would become one of the best-known songs of the year. It showcased the somewhat grittier vocals of Cornell, who sounded as if he'd been heavily on the whiskey and cigarettes since his musical sabbatical. On the negative side, this could have been construed by critics as him struggling to find the power that his once untouchable voice exuded. 'Cochise' was undoubtedly a difficult song to sing, covering a husky verse and bawled chorus before breaking down into an almost spoken interlude, before Cornell screams the song back into life again. Difficult to produce but memorable instantly, this was perhaps the greatest song on the debut album (self-titled for simplicity).

It was also memorable for the incendiary music video made to accompany the song which was directed by Mark Romanek. To accompany the striking cover art for the album, the band used a plethora of fireworks to introduce Audioslave and 'Cochise' to the world, with the band playing on top of a construction tower during the video and entirely lit by a dramatic fireworks display. People living in the Sepulveda Dam area of Los Angeles saw and heard the masses of explosions and assumed they might be under attack from terrorists. Even without trying, Tom Morello and Co. could incite panic in the general public!

The likes of 'Show Me How To Live' featured a riff Morello could have played slightly faster to fit RATM, with a somnambulant drum beat which again, if faster, could have been a Rage song. But with the slower beat, the song moulded around Cornell's soulful vocals, bringing an altogether different vibe. Though he rarely hit the ascension of his previous vocal work, it was clear this man could sing for his supper. He'd simply refined his style, perhaps making it easier for himself to not go all out at any point, though the chorus to 'Show Me...' comes close. The comparison with Zack De La Rocha could not have been more opposite, despite the recognised backing of the RATM troupe. Cornell couldn't and didn't want to rap, instead crooning, screaming or shouting his way through proceedings. Likewise, De La Rocha rarely sang, more versed in the hip-hop mentality and taking an obvious stance against the basics of the rock genre. Here was a different outlet for Messrs Wilk, Commerford and Morello and one they ably adapted to. It was as if they had been a melodic rock band their entire career.

Yet one always felt this assertion was something they were merely toying with, almost threatening to pull out at any stage. In many ways, they were still assaulting the mainstream mentality, even when playing in a largely mainstream band. The video for 'Show Me How To Live' was reputedly banned by MTV because it featured Chris Cornell in a high speed car chase where he was running various police vehicles off the road. Subliminally these artists were still rebelling at every opportunity.

To some it seemed this was a style of music the band were not completely well versed in, with several filler tracks making up the album (though in true RATM tradition, the album became better with more time spent in its company). When the band truly fired on all cylinders they were a joy to behold. 'Like A Stone' was not the noisiest track on the album but it showcased the band's true potential. A cunning, emotional rollercoaster bathed in soul, like all the best Cornell-fronted material whether it be 'Blow Up The Outside World' or 'Can't Change Me'.

And Tom Morello excelled with one of his most moving solos to date, still utilising his experimental technique but underlining it with maximum feel for the beauty of the song. As the second single from the album, 'Like A Stone' became the most successful release, reaching #1 on the *Billboard* Mainstream Rock Tracks chart as well as the Modern Rock Tracks chart. It also peaked at #31 on the *Billboard* Hot 100 chart.

The lyrics within the album were typical of the ambiguous spirituality and personal fancies Cornell was noted for. In fact they were so non-specific it was one of the clearest areas of opposition to the work that RATM were famous for. But this was not a political band and while Audioslave started a crusade for music rather than a message, Tom Morello expanded his politics through his organisation Axis Of Justice (more on which later).

"And there he found the spark to set this fucker off," Cornell says in one of his more memorable lines in the hefty rock funk of 'Set It Off'. Cornell would be criticised for his lyrics, but this was unfair. Given De La Rocha's political stance and deft dalliances with causes he could wrap in poetical fury, Cornell was never going to compare. Besides, his ambiguous lyrics had always been the source of confusion for many fans. His art was unique and not clearly definable. Some people just have to accept that not every lyricist is direct or clear in their intentions and expressions. Some emotions are subliminal and only come out in their performance. Cornell was a soulful singer who exorcised his inner demons in his emotional larynx outbursts such as the touching swathe of 'Shadow On The Sun', again blended perfectly with Morello's sumptuous guitar which made mincemeat of the typical solo, artfully creating a sonic purge of emotion with the merest of guitar work. Somewhat surprisingly this evocative number was not chosen as a single.

175

'I Am The Highway' was released as a single however. This track, more surreptitious than its predecessor on the album, was a song for driving to, ironically enough, evoking truck stops and cheap motels as a daring vigilante drives cross country. This was perhaps the greatest indication of the long path the ex-members of Rage Against The Machine had travelled. Here they stood at the precipice of modern, almost *MOR* rock. Yet, just because they were not extrapolating political verse from their singer did not make them any less meaningful, and 'I Am The Highway' was a poignant, slow building moment with long drawn out verses and the crackling acoustic guitar refrains which brought to mind long dusty roads gently caressed by scattered tumbleweeds. In this song, as on many throughout the album, simplicity and inherent emotion are the order of the day. And as the band seemed to discover, writing songs more simply and with less emphasis on hard riffing was in many ways harder than plugging in and screaming away.

Elsewhere 'Exploder' was a slow burner, erupting in a torrent of Morello six string abuse, with the emphasis particularly driving the song on the bending of the note accompanying the last word of each chorus line. There was the morose march of 'Light My Way', the unremarkable 'Bring 'Em Back Alive' and the mournful sub-acoustic album closer 'The Last Remaining Light'. Some songs were a little disappointing with their simplistic choruses and predictable pattern, but then there was subtle beauty in simplicity and longevity in songs which took a while to hammer home their point. Yet as can often be the case, when an album crams in most of its singles in the early part of proceedings, towards the end the songs can lose their way.

Audioslave was welcomed as a whole, selling 162,000 copies in its first week of release in America alone and finding its way to Number 7 in the *Billboard* chart. Within a month the album achieved gold status (500,000 sales) and by 2006 it would turn triple platinum having sold more than three millions copies worldwide.

It later emerged that during the recording sessions for the album, Chris Cornell had been in rehab for two months mostly concerning alcohol (this wasn't helped by splitting from his wife;

there were reports of issues other than alcohol too). The need for rehab was yet another bizarre parallel with Metallica and yet came after the intervention of Phil Towle. During one of Audioslave's shows Cornell claimed that the rest of the band had "saved his life" during this period.

In August 2003, the musicians in Audioslave reacquainted themselves with Lollapalooza, this time with Chris Cornell in tow. There were no incendiary incidents to speak of, just a great show and positive reviews. Just before this, the band had released a self-titled DVD featuring all their videos to date as well as footage from one of their earliest public performances where they had played on *The David Letterman Show* in 2002.

The Audioslave live experience was not about being so high and mighty that the band would insist on only playing material the four of them had created. Rather than avoid their past, the dual careers of Morello and Co. as well as Chris Cornell, were embraced and merged together to create a monster set list. This consisted of different songs on different nights taking in whatever the band felt like. But Cornell managed to front the Rage Against The Machine material without a hitch and, of course, the band could play the backing to certain Soundgarden songs with equal sincerity.

At varying stages the band played the likes of RATM's 'Killing In The Name', 'Bulls On Parade' and 'Sleep Now In The Fire' as well as Soundgarden's 'Spoonman', 'Black Hole Sun' and 'Fell On Black Days'. "We're going deeper into the catalogues of both Rage and Soundgarden," Morello told Adam Bulger. "It's really exciting for us to play them and the room just explodes. When we decided to look at the material from our past bands, we didn't just decide to do it, it had to sound great. Chris really owns those songs that we've chosen to do. It's not the least bit strange. It's just awesome. Every night when we make up a set list, we're able to draw from 11 multi-platinum albums. Very few bands can do that."

It was a stretch to say Cornell was performing the RATM classics with the same gusto as Zack De La Rocha. His contribution to some of Rage's most potent tracks was strained in places and down right out of place in others. Those songs were not meant for a conventional singer and whenever Cornell tried to emit the force of shouted or spoken sections it did not resonate with the fury originally intended with the material. It just went to prove how unique De La Rocha was and how it probably wouldn't have mattered who the band had brought in to replace the rapper, had they gone on to continue as RATM and play more of their back catalogue it would have spelled disaster. The band clearly did the right thing by avoiding the responsibility of carrying on RATM in its usual form. No one came close to De La Rocha and, if nothing else, the Cornell-fronted version of Rage merely showed he was better off sticking to the style of singing he knew best. To be fair to Cornell, it was an unenviable position to be in.

Back in the days of Rage Against The Machine, Tom Morello had previously told one interviewer, "Creatively, the slow pace of recording and touring is very frustrating for me. I would love to make a record every year, maybe two records every year, and tour the world and play in front of our amazing fans much more often than we do. But unfortunately within our band there are very different creative metabolisms, and some of us just work more slowly than others. The upside is that I work with three incredible musicians who make the powerful music that is a unique product of our chemistry."

By the time Audioslave had finished off the touring for their debut album, it was two and a half years before their second album hit the shelves, though it was still quicker than the average RATM turnaround and this certainly pleased Tom Morello. The band spent most of 2004 taking a break and slowly working on the follow-up album, though for some songs it was a case of tweaking quality material unused on the debut album, as well as working on new material written during the Lollapalooza tour and beyond. Tom Morello worked on Axis Of Justice and other political interests while, after his divorce was finalised, Chris Cornell remarried to a publicist named Vicky Karayiannis, based in Paris, who he had met while touring Europe with Audioslave.

Three weeks before the release of their next album, Audioslave played a gig in Cuba on May 6, 2005, in front of 65,000 rabid fans, where they debuted three new tracks from their forthcoming set. This was captured for posterity on the *Live In Cuba* DVD released later that year. Not only was the concert special for the new material, but Audioslave just happened to be the first American hard rock band to play in the country.

"It wasn't something we'll soon forget," Tom Morello said with some understatement in *Alternative Press*. "We had wanted to do it for some time. Even back in the Rage days we had talked about it, but we hadn't been able to get it together. As you probably know, there's an embargo against Cuba. US citizens can't travel there, let alone bring a rock band with a PA system and all that. It took a lot of perseverance. Finally, the US Treasury Department and Castro himself had to sign off on it. It was billed as a cultural exchange. Before the concert, we were treated to seeing some amazing experiences. We saw Cuban artists, amazing musicians just jamming on the street. We went to this free music school that used to be an élitist country club before the revolution where there were these jaw-dropping jazz musicians. It really humbled us and made us want to give our all when we played."

With no mere hint of protest, Audioslave played at the La Tribuna Antiimperialista José Martí, which was purpose-built in 2000 for mass protests against the US government. The band arrived two days before their scheduled performance to take in the beauty of Havana and spend some time with local youngsters and musicians. Tom Morello insisted this was not a political statement, merely an attempt to build bridges between the two countries – and perhaps also to show the similarities between the two cultures and that music could transcend all boundaries. Chris Cornell even hoped the concert would "help to open the musical borders between our two countries."

As mentioned, the band used a combination of pre-existing material and new ideas to construct their second album, which was to be titled *Out Of Exile*. It was released on May 23 and 24, 2005, in Europe and the US respectively. It was the first and only one of the band's albums to top the *Billboard* chart. Lead single 'Be Yourself' was an understated yet brilliant call to arms with the title speaking for itself. Fans were invited to send in their pictures of the band for the front cover art, twenty-four of which were used for the 7" single release.

179

The record saw the band entering even lighter waters with an almost middle of the road anthem. Many critics were instantly vocal that this was not the expected or accepted direction for a band whose members had once been so feared by the mainstream. The song was cast as 'bland' in several quarters but to many ears was one of the band's best tunes to date. It might have been better as the second single from the album but instead, album opener 'Your Time Has Come' was released subsequently. The song featured a typically driving Morello riff and a lively vocal outpouring from Cornell. There was a mixture of great rock touches, from the bridge section which recalled Pearl Jam, to the cowbell used in the middle of the song, which recalled just about every Eighties rock act with maybe a hint of sarcasm.

Thematically it was one of the more interesting Audioslave topics. As Chris Cornell would attest, the song's inspiration came from the superb 'People Who Died' by The Jim Carroll Band. Jim Carroll is a poet and writer who is most famous for his memoirs *The Basketball Diaries*, which were made into a film in 1995. The book details his growing up and addiction to heroin. 'People Who Died' was a poignant memorial to people Carroll grew up with who had died as young men and women due to everything from suicide to drug overdoses. "It's a bunch of references to people that I knew that were younger than me who've been dead for years and years, up to a couple of years ago," Cornell clarified regarding 'Your Time Has Come', "it is also about people who killed themselves before their time has come."

Like Carroll's song, Audioslave also refer to the Vietnam war. The first line was a reference to the Vietnam Veterans Memorial (located in Washington D.C.). In yet another connection with Metallica, the band were criticised by many fans of Hetfield and Co. worldwide that they had aped the riff to Metallica's 'Bad Seed' in their song. Despite this common criticism on forums and chat rooms all over the world, Audioslave has yet to comment on the similarities.

'Doesn't Remind Me' was a gorgeous flowing song which built up around a chord structure and bass accompaniment very reminiscent of Pearl Jam. Even Cornell's low-slung vocals were evocative of his friend Eddie Vedder, with the verse re-enacting the

Temple Of The Dog material the two had collaborated on. "We were really on a roll in the rehearsal studio, and ideas were flowing very freely, and that one was just a simple chord progression that had great dynamics and rocked pretty hard," Morello said. "It's one of my favourite songs on the record." Though it was a simple song it seemed to show the progression from album one to two, whereby Audioslave could now write those basic song structures and make them emphatic. By now they had perfectly adjusted to life as a mainstream rock band, though there were the inevitable sounds and noises in the Morello guitar solo to reference his past. Still 'Doesn't Remind Me' featured one of his more straightforward hard rock solos.

Chris Cornell was even taken aback at the simplicity of the song. "I was out of town, and these guys recorded that and a bunch of other stuff on a tape," he explained, "and when I returned we were working on different things on the tape and then started playing that one and I thought, 'Wow, I'm surprised we're working on this, like somebody wanted to do such a simple chord progression in a song'. 'Cause personally I would not have chosen that, which is part of the reason I love being in a band and collaborating with other people."

One of the band's strengths was that despite the majority of their material falling squarely into the rock genre, they could aptly switch moods from track to track and not seem out of place, so from 'Doesn't Remind Me' they could also rock out on 'Your Time Has Come' or segue into the hard rocking thump of 'Drown Me Slowly', the husky Cornell emitting his more typical Soundgarden throat tricks.

It would be pushing it to suggest the preceding Audioslave debut was a classic but it was certainly a strong record, especially for a first collaboration; yet *Out Of Exile* was instantly head and shoulders above its predecessor and whereas the debut lost its way at some stages, this one didn't falter too often. Equally, in line with their previous recordings, these musicians gave supreme value for money, recording 12 songs all of which required some time and effort to became fully acquainted with and ultimately releasing another timeless album which could hold its own for many years to come. It wasn't all just about carefully constructed pop rock;

there were doses of heaviness which recalled the darker era of Soundgarden, such as the screeching lurch of 'The Worm'. This song fell into the upbeat stomp of 'Man Or Animal', taking the listener on another journey and solidifying this band's ability to administer the pure beauty of a hard rock song as required.

One of the biggest benefits of having Chris Cornell as a frontman was his ability to play various roles within the same band, from heavy metal screamer to lightly dusted crooner, and sometimes his moody delivery covered several bases within the space of the same song, never once losing its power or driving force. 'Man Or Animal' was one of those moments, and a particular highlight of the album.

The album went from strength to strength with the sublime beauty of 'Yesterday To Tomorrow' which seemed a certain choice for a single, except no one took the bait and it puzzlingly remained an album-only track. Chris Cornell was now a completely different singer to the one who barked his way through several Soundgarden albums, and he had tried to head this way before on his solo album and to an extent his work on the Temple Of The Dog record. But, here, he finally made the perfect recording of the pop rock hybrid, emotionally charging the power ballad sweetness/inspiration of this truly immense work.

'Dandelion' was one of the only tracks on the album to reference the Seventies rock scene, with the gently hummed chorus and jangly Morello guitar, this was a perfect song for either personal introspection or a bright summer's day without a care in the world, a hugely difficult balance to strike. '#1 Zero' showcased the Cornell larynx to its full reach, again with a notable influence from several decades of rock. The singer was alleged to have improved his voice in giving up alcohol and cigarettes and whether it was due to this or not, the album seemed to be better for Cornell's breakthrough.

'The Curse' was a somewhat anti-climactic end to the album, with no real direction or purpose. Yet overall album number two was a supreme success and cemented Audioslave's place in the modern era of rock. They were not just one of the top selling bands of modern times, they were one of the greatest.

Many critics wondered how Tom Morello could completely withdraw from the political arena, as they saw it, to focus on a band where protest music and education were not the prominent building blocks. However, to augment his politicised cravings, Tom Morello had formed the aforementioned Axis Of Justice organisation along with System Of A Down's Serj Tankian. The non-profit AOJ organisation was formed with the purpose of bringing "together musicians, fans of music, and grassroots political organizations to fight for social justice," as it states on the official AOJ website – www.axisofjustice.org. "We aim to build a bridge between fans of music around the world and local political organisations to effectively organise around issues of peace, human rights, and economic justice." The website gives several pointers as to how readers can get involved in specific causes and provides an extensive list of suggested reading. AOJ excels with the inclusion of a radio network which has featured some of the most prominent political commentators of the modern day – from Michael Moore and Noam Chomsky to lesser known but no less appealing figures including documentary maker Robert Greenwald (who produced a superb documentary on the high street food chain Wal-Mart – *Wal-Mart: The High Cost Of Low Price*) to singer and activist Billy Bragg. The musical connection of the network was something to admire in particular.

"The purpose is to expose our audience to rebel music of different genres and let people know there's a tether between Bob Dylan and Rage and Pete Seeger and System Of A Down and Public Enemy," Morello explained. This desire to combine revolutionary artists (and just straightforward great rock bands whether it be Guns N' Roses or Queen) in a melting pot of educational comment was commendable and all the brilliant shows broadcast are available at the website for free download.

Chapter Fifteen
Stage Fight

By the time of Audioslave's third album, the cracks were starting to show. When they had first assaulted the mainstream music industry, they were a relatively unknown quantity – a strange concoction and an exciting proposition. Tom Morello successfully adapted his guitar style to suit a mainstream rock band and Chris Cornell streamlined his vocals to front a cross between Soundgarden and his *Euphoria Morning* material. Arguably this was still the case for the new *Revelations* album, which was released on September 5, 2006.

Yet somehow there was a spiral dysfunction within the camp, something even Chris Cornell would later allude to. *Kerrang!* called the album "turgid" and compared the material to that of Whitesnake (and not in a good way). It was ironic then that the album featured a number of tracks which ranked alongside Audioslave's best material.

The title track was a sumptuous, free flowing sway through contemporary soft rock, featuring one of Morello's most understated guitar licks. It was immediately obvious the guitar was placed further behind other elements with greater emphasis on the vocals and melodies. Yet the solo was a gorgeous trail through expected Morello territory, albeit over all too quickly. 'One And The Same' was a bristling waltz of low-fi guitar funk and almost subliminal vocals, Cornell sounding huskier than ever. The highlight of the song was the combination of the Morello six string antics and the accompanying Cornell drawl, drooling the words, "just like blood and rain, love and pain are one and the same."

Though it was implausibly simple and predictable, the

immediacy of 'Sound Of A Gun' suggested a future Audioslave favourite, sitting betwixt the alternative roots of the band with the mainstream, catchy radio chorus ethic of their modern day transformation. 'Original Fire' was a clear standout track, and the only song to truly reference the Seventies rock influence supposedly inherent. The upbeat vocals suited Cornell and make for a welcome break from the usual Audioslave formula. Taking on a virtual gospel quality, this was truly great sing-a-long music.

The swaggering underestimation of 'Broken City' showed Audioslave were now playing with textures and dynamics in a far subtler way than their previous output suggested, from RATM to the early 'Slave albums. The song hulked through a veritable treasure trove of funky guitar flecks and an almost sluggish Cornell croon. Not immediate, nor incendiary but highly enjoyable all the same. After this track, however, the impact of the album subsided and the remainder blurred into a less than inspired hotch potch of varying rock derivations.

It was only due to the fact the 'filler' material on the album was indeed quite turgid that the album as a whole was poorly received. It also seemed more to do with the fact that the media, and perhaps even certain sections of the fan base, were tired of Audioslave and wanted Rage Against The Machine back. It was an insinuation the entire 'Slave brigade seemed to be aware of and – perhaps – even in agreement with, as their subsequent actions and words would suggest.

Perhaps the band was simply pushing the mainstream rock band ethic a touch too far. They created Audioslave nation – a fictional utopian island (in the South Pacific) based on the album cover art. This was promoted and marketed via Google Earth. Several songs on the album were also used in a slew of mainstream products, from the video game soundtrack to *Madden NFL 07* (with 'Revelations') to the inclusion of 'Shape Of Things To Come' and 'Wide Awake' in the *Miami Vice* movie.

Was it necessary to stretch the boundaries of the band to feature on a video game? Of course, there are no laws against doing what you want and the seed of rebellion is born from doing just that, but cynics suggested there surely had to be some limits as to how far the members were compliant in working with (rather than within) the establishment. Though the third album would sell well in its first week of release, it dropped considerably after that and ironically signalled the death knell for the band, despite their huge marketing campaign and wealth of promotion. The notion that the album was, as Tom Morello put it, "Led Zeppelin meets Earth, Wind & Fire" seemed a touch too far for even the most staunch supporters of the band. Still, though many would lazily contest the album was everything from "funk" to "R&B" it was only in disparate drips that these elements showed their face. For the most part, this was simply middle-of-the-road rock. However, the band seemed to be an on-going concern despite the fact Cornell was aiming to record a second solo album and Tom Morello wanted to concentrate on his The Nightwatchman project.

The Nightwatchman evolved as a vent for Morello's political thoughts and feelings, though was initially planned as something of a side-project, to play a few low key shows here and there. Instead, it became one of Morello's most ambitious undertakings to date, and something which few truly seemed to understand – the album has at the time of writing sold less than 25,000 copies and became the first album Morello had been involved with since Lock Up's *Something Bitchy This Way Comes* to not go multi-platinum. Reviews didn't help, uninspired journalists seemingly caught in a web of iPod generation head-scratching or the flip side – a generation yielded from the Springsteen era and unable to give praise where it's due to a guitarist who was by now better known for axe effects than his ability to pen a decent tune.

To offset his basic rock affections in Audioslave, Morello decided he wanted to strip it down and perform acoustic folk by himself. He started with a show in a Los Angeles coffeehouse before an intimate crowd but was soon enlisted to support Billy Bragg on his 'Tell Us The Truth' tour. Though all The Nightwatchman's songs were present and correct, Morello wasn't initially intending to put them down for posterity yet when he was asked to provide a song for the *Fahrenheit 9/11* soundtrack, along with his old friend Zack De La Rocha, Morello obliged and recorded 'No One Left', a mournful dedication to the victims of the 9/11 attack and the on-going casualties of the unjustifiable war. However, it would take three years for Morello to polish off a full album. After this he would also contribute a track to another Michael Moore film, the *Sicko* documentary, released in 2007.

Some may assume it's easier to put together songs when it's just one man and a guitar but as any experienced musician will tell you, it can be harder. Sure, you can strum a few chords and hum here and there, but to make truly memorable music with such limited resources takes talent and perspiration – something Morello possessed in abundance and was not afraid of. It took him a while but the thirteen tracks which made up *One Man Revolution* were studious, considered and, yes, revolutionary. Sadly, the album seemed to pass many people by – perhaps as a consequence of not referring to it as an album by Tom Morello, perhaps as a consequence of being assaulted not by amplified guitar but by lamenting ballads best heard by night lantern.

Drawing on all the inspiration of political songsters of the past – from Phil Ochs to Woody Guthrie – the album was also a pleasant nod to the alternative country scene and referenced everyone from Willard Grant Conspiracy to Calexico. And there was the Johnny Cash inspired emotional delivery which Morello possessed. His voice was deep yet clear and emotive and carried the barest bones of a song in some cases, raising hairs on arms and neck as he let the music and words take on a life of their own.

The album could be taken either as a soothing comedown from the frantic world of rock, or as a piece of insightful poetry set to some truly inspiring and beautiful music. Either way, this was a highlight of Morello's career. If Morello could create this kind of supremely memorable material with limited resources, accompanied only by his beat up guitar and soulful voice, then Audioslave was always about more than one man.

Morello called The Nightwatchman "The black Robin Hood of 21st Century music" and "a reaction against illicit wars, a reaction against first strikes, torture, secret prisons, spying illegally on American citizens. It's a reaction against war crimes, and it's a reaction against a few corporations that grow rich off this illicit war while people beg for food in the city streets. To me, it seems that the world needs songs of rebellion and revolution right now. It's exciting."

Instantly, the thrum of opener 'California's Dark' showed the listener this was a vastly different proposition from either Rage Against The Machine or Audioslave and, as Morello himself suggested, it was indeed exciting to hear a modern day political poet and artist produce such a blatant set of revolutionary material. Far better when the lyrics were straightforward and easily identified. The opening track is more of a plaintive introduction and was swiftly followed by one of the best tracks on the album, the vibrant title track.

The album was produced by Brendan O'Brien and he also contributed backing vocals and extra instrumentation as on the title track where he sang and played piano. This was one of the strongest, catchiest tracks on the album and the perfect demonstration of The Nightwatchman rhetoric.

The subtle beauty of 'Let Freedom Ring' shows Morello could easily adapt his style to any form of poetical protest, his voice straining with emotion and carrying the lovelorn ballad. The song brought to mind the subtler vocal moments of both Nick Cave or Mark Lanegan and this song alone should have marked Morello out as a leading contender in the world of American alternative music, be it alternative country or pure indie rock.

The highlight of the album however had to be the Gaelic inspired 'The Road I Must Travel' complete with synthesized bagpipes. Blessed with a Scottish flair (and not just due to the bagpipes) the track could have been a song by Big Country or even The Proclaimers, stretching back also to old Scottish folk material such as Billy Connolly and Gerry Rafferty's The Humblebums. Dutifully sing-a-long in its approach and resplendent with bittersweet lyrics, this was Morello at his solo best. The guitar Morello held aloft on the front cover of the album is emblazoned with the slogan – 'Whatever it takes', signifying his intent to keep pushing until the world changes.

'House Gone Up In Flames' was evocative of Dire Straits, Morello's voice taking on a Mark Knopfler style emotion, evoking the likes of 'The Man's Too Strong' from their 1985 *Brothers In Arms* album. Certain songs were less than impressive though, following a predictable route and blending into the background, particularly 'The Dark Clouds Above', 'The Garden Of Gethsemane' and 'Flesh Shapes The Day'.

Yet as the album neared its end, there are several potent, impassioned tracks which make up for the occasional loss of momentum. 'Maximum Firepower' is rugged and thrusting, only pausing for breath in the understated chorus. It also recalls an underrated batch of songwriters, Morello coming off like a furious Justin Sullivan, the leader of New Model Army.

'Union Song' was not the most potent musical concoction on the album but was defiant in its lyrical content, name-checking other political activist singers and referencing the sweatshop labour epidemic and the power of workers' unions. Album closer 'Until The End' was a sombre, reflective tune perfectly in keeping with the unhurried acoustic hue of which Morello has by now proved himself wholly adept. Reminiscent of the modern work of Johnny Cash, the song was Morello's dedication to those who have been locked away unashamedly and unjustly – despite running at over four minutes, it was over all too quickly.

And so *One Man Revolution* drew to a close with a plaintive strum of an acoustic just as it had begun. There were no amplified guitar histrionics or clever and inventive tricks with knobs and tools, just one man and a basic acoustic guitar. Morello turned the notion of being a one trick pony on its head, and truly personified the idiom – less is more.

For Audioslave, there were inevitable suggestions that a split was imminent but the band denied this. Cornell even went as far as to say, "We hear rumours that Audioslave is breaking up all the time, I always just ignore them."

Yet, on February 15, 2007, Cornell himself announced he had left the band, despite apparently not informing his band mates of the decision first. In his official statement, Cornell said, "Due to irresolvable personality conflicts as well as musical differences, I am permanently leaving the band Audioslave. I wish the other three members nothing but the best in all of their future endeavours." He told *Entertainment Weekly* that the rest of the band "found out with everybody else, and I haven't heard from them at all since."

Clearly the differences were irreconcilable and seemed to refer to the same problems hinted at years previously when Cornell was first rumoured to be leaving the group. In a *New York Post* news piece the premise was that the decision to disband was purely financial. "Tom and I did have communications about the fact that I was gonna go make a record," Cornell himself said to MTV, "and that I was tired of what ended up seeming like political negotiations toward how we were gonna do Audioslave business and getting nowhere with it."

There were suggestions that arguments had rumbled along about who wrote the most material, an age-old thorn in many band's sides. It has to be stated that all music from the band was credited as being written by the band as a collective.

Speaking to *Entertainment Weekly*, Cornell elaborated on his reason for leaving the band. "It comes down to this: we came from different bands that had pretty tumultuous existences," he said. "We agreed to do Audioslave under the premise that it was going to be harmonious and fun for everybody, and as soon as it wasn't that way anymore, I didn't want to do it. We started having problems from day one. There was, of course, this awkwardness where you have a 12-year relationship as a band and then an outsider comes in, particularly one that had a 15-year relationship with another band. For me, it was great creatively, but personally, it was like suddenly having step-parents. And as hard as we all worked at trying to respect different opinions and perspectives, when it came to the inner workings of the band, they had their way of doing things and I had mine. And they seemed to be at odds with one another, too."

The phrase 'creative differences' is uttered so often by bands who split that it has lost its meaning. Some phrases describe the situation so perfectly and exactly that they can be used in a multitude of circumstances with seemingly little accuracy. But in this case, it seemed a little of everything, from personal and creative differences to management and financial issues. Either way, it was everything a rock band was supposed to override and where it was no longer fun for Cornell, you can safely assume the musical trio didn't see much enjoyment in the associating business anymore either.

And though he seemed to no longer be close friends with his ex-band mates, Chris Cornell hinted that he knew what was coming next when he also told *Entertainment Weekly*, "Seeing Rage live was the reason that Audioslave existed! It's why I wanted to get in a room with those guys because they were some of the best performances I'd ever seen. And a part of me thinks they should still be a band."

Chapter Sixteen
Reunited We Stand

With Audioslave behind them, there was a persistent rumour following Messrs Morello, Wilk and Commerford concerning the reformation of Rage Against The Machine. If ever there was a band who seemed unlikely to reunite, it was surely RATM. Not only were there the well-publicised spats within the group which had contributed to their original split – but times had changed and the ex-musical trio who had backed De La Rocha in Rage had since experienced life in a major, far more commercial rock outfit. It was an intoxicating experience and one they perhaps did not want to completely leave behind. Still, Rage brought its own success and notoriety and though they sounded far from mainstream, they managed to permeate the very centre of the commercial whirlpool, such was their popularity.

Yet the question still remained – why would they even get back together? And secondly, would Zack De La Rocha actually want to do it? Was he in the right headspace and would he think there was any reason to start Rage all over again?

The vocalist was well known for his seclusion and interest in activism above all else, but even by his standards he had been very quiet since the RATM split. The solo album he had worked on for so long was still missing in action, seemingly never likely to see the light of day – which would surely be a great loss. De La Rocha was in collaboration with many artists whom few RATM fans were probably interested in, perhaps not being familiar with them at all. There were modern dance icons such as Roni Size, DJ Shadow and Dan The Automator as well as Cypress Hill's DJ Muggs, soul writer James Poyser and jazz/soul artist Questlove, of The Roots.

This writer has heard some of the tracks that Zack collaborated on with various cohorts and can safely say it is essentially hip-hop for the most part. There are a few gems, covering bases as broad as classic early rap and yet referencing modern artists such as Non Phixion. There is the humorous, quirky swagger of 'C.I.A. (Criminals In Action)', a collaboration with an artist De La Rocha especially admires, KRS-1. The song even samples KRS's own 'Sound Of Da Police' with its familiar and mocking refrain of "Woop-woop! That's the sound of da police!"

The collaboration with Floridian duo Dead Prez is understandable given their alliances. The group have a strong standing in underground hip-hop circles and their criticisms of the establishment are well known. Like Rage Against The Machine in fact, they focus on everything from the prison system and capitalist globalist control to police brutality and mainstream media repression.

De La Rocha also appeared on 'Mumia 911', essentially a lengthy diatribe supporting Mumia Abu-Jamal and making sardonic references to his 'crimes'. There are numerous rappers in attendance with the RATM vocalist only making a relatively short contribution, though his lyrics are incendiary. The song also featured the likes of Chuck D and Pharoahe Monch but was far more memorable for the sentiment and message than the music.

There were also actual appearances on albums released to the public, though both were less than memorable. De La Rocha appeared on Roni Size's (a Bristolian DJ and producer) *In The Mode* album in 2000 on a track called 'Centre Of The Storm'. Though overall a drum and bass recording, *In The Mode* was buoyed by the presence of De La Rocha who made the song his own, rapping over the frantic beat. Few drum and bass standards were geared towards a straightforward verse-chorus rhetoric but this came close.

Two years later he contributed a stunted part of the Blackalicious song 'Release' which appeared on their *Blazing Arrow* album. Zack raps the "release" mantra in the background to the speedy rapping skills of MC Gift Of Gab. The song came in three parts and was lengthy at 9:26 but De La Rocha only appeared in the first part and literally contributed one word.

Clearly many of the musicians and producers De La Rocha collaborated with for his mooted solo album are all linked and associated amongst themselves. On the *Blazing Arrow* album, many of those who were assisting the RATM vocalist make an appearance, from James Poyser to DJ Shadow. De La Rocha also lent his weighty name to the soundtrack for the Michael Moore film, *Fahrenheit 9/11* – a worthy documentary exposing the reasons and methods behind the 9/11 tragedy. The song, 'We Want It All' was one of his most straightforward vocal performances to date, with a simple yet strong backing riff reminiscent of hardcore protagonists Girls Against Boys. Like that very band 'We Want It All' is somewhat distorted, almost messy, yet carefully composed and, ultimately, inspiring.

On top of this there was a full album of material De La Rocha recorded with Nine Inch Nails' Trent Reznor but refused to release, which who no one aside from those in the studio at the time have even heard or are indeed likely to hear. Reznor himself said the songs were "excellent" but went on to say the RATM vocalist wasn't ready to release them.

It goes without saying that De La Rocha is a livewire, fiercely independent and creatively unpredictable. He also had the difficulties combining his activist stance with life in a popular rock band – something which if the band were to reform he would have to reconcile.

One song which did see release was a collaboration with DJ Shadow entitled 'March Of Death'. This was initially released for free online. Cuts and beats back the ferocious rap, somewhat diluting its power. As usual, even with the most faithful of hip-hop paeans, this could be reconstructed as a rock song; its arguable that 'March Of Death' would have been far better as a straightforward rock song – and perhaps would have garnered greater attention.

The lyrics concerned the hostile entry into Iraq of American forces, a situation which had been ongoing and building momentum since the September 11 attacks in 2001. Many artists were opposed to the war and many of those were not afraid to say so. Yet it was often as if their contributions criticising the American administration and in particular George W. Bush were nothing more than a contrived way of jumping on the bandwagon. It was easy to criticise a numbskull leader and who, with an ounce of humanity, could really speak up for justification of the war? Yet somehow certain bands seemed to garner attention just because they were suddenly interested in politics and felt the need to say something.

When Zack De La Rocha installed his opinion into public consciousness, it was naturally more erudite and on the button than the majority of his musical peers. This was his *passion*, always had been; he'd been doing this for years. The vocalist broke his media silence with an impassioned statement regarding the song and its focus. On the official RATM website De La Rocha questioned the motives and focus of the Bush administration's policy in Iraq. Writing with great feeling and knowledge, De La Rocha is as compelling a writer as he is an orator.

Perhaps world events would shape a proposed RATM comeback, or maybe it was just meant to be? Still it was surprising when American music trade magazine *Billboard* reported that within the music industry there were indeed serious rumours of an impending reformation.

… And so it proved, as word quickly spread across the internet when the Coachella festival in California suddenly listed Rage Against The Machine as one of their acts and simultaneously confirmed the rumours. Rage were to headline the closing night of the festival on April 29, 2007. Tom Morello had indicated something could be afoot regarding RATM when he gave an interview to *Kerrang!* solely about the band, despite having Audioslave's new record to promote. He told Ben Myers, "Honestly, with Rage, there were few moments of pure, unadulterated joy. A dark cloud followed us everywhere and for nearly a decade we had been about to break-up any day. It was nothing new to us because that was the life we were leading: one of heroic music and great personal tension … We'd sold millions but we had also demolished our personal relationships along the way."

Yet, even with the hint of enduring passion for his old band, it still needed a catalyst to set the wheels in motion. And it happened when De La Rocha and Morello were working voluntarily for the South Central Farmers, a group of workers from a non-profit farm that serves the community of the notorious gang area.

Ben Myers wrote, "Facing eviction from a wealthy landowner, the 'South Central Farmers Feeding Families' organisation was formed in 2004 from some 350 local impoverished family members and fund-raising to buy the land back began. Both Morello and De La Rocha offered support alongside celebrities such as Willie Nelson, Flea and Leonardo DiCaprio, the front man visiting the site where he performed with the popular traditional Mexican group Son De Madera at a 'Save The Farm' rally."

"This must rank as one of the most understated rock star comebacks of all time," reported the *LA Times*. "De La Rocha – his dreadlocks replaced by a frizzy Afro, his electric guitar by a small Mexican jarana – walked casually onstage in the sweltering Hall of North American Mammals to the cheers of fans crammed between diorama exhibits of wildlife along each side."

Chris Cornell was interviewed for *Entertainment Weekly* and asked whether the reformation of RATM had affected his decision to quit Audioslave, but according to the vocalist the two were not connected. "Not much, really," he responded. "After the third Audioslave record was done, I started an album on my own and made a decision to spend time away from the band. And it was anybody's guess what that time apart would create. But suddenly, my life was in order and I was enjoying every aspect of making music, especially being able to work at home with my family, without the constant give and take. Musically, I felt like I could go in any direction I wanted, and that brought me to the conclusion that it wasn't something that I wanted to do anymore."

For the return of Rage Against The Machine on August 24, 2007, Mary Morello made a return too, introducing the band to the lucky throng in attendance, who were to witness history. Not only did Rage play a sterling set, turning back time as if they'd never been away, but they also used the opportunity to instantly make an impassioned statement once again.

During the feedback wails of 'Wake Up', De La Rocha referred to Noam Chomsky when he said, "A good friend of ours once said that if the same laws were applied to US presidents as were applied to the Nazis after World War II, every single one of them, every last rich white one of them from Truman on, would have been hung to death and shot and this current administration is no exception. They should be hung, and tried, and shot. As any war criminal should be."

Consequently Rage stirred the establishment as never before and found their way onto the coffee table news forum that is *Fox News*. On the programme *Hannity & Colmes*, a clip of the De La Rocha speech was aired while the 'BREAKING NEWS' headline stated, "Rock group Rage Against The Machine says Bush admin should be shot." Conservative attorney Ann Coulter said, "They're losers, their fans are losers, and there's a lot of violence coming from the left-wing."

Unsurprisingly, this did not sit well with Zack De La Rocha and when RATM co-headlined the *Rock The Bells* hip-hop festival in late July, he again spoke during the performance of 'Wake Up'. "A couple of months ago, those fascist motherfuckers at the Fox News Network attempted to pin this band into a corner by suggesting that we said that the president should be assassinated," he spat. "Nah, what we said was that he should be brought to trial as war criminal and hung and shot. *That* is what we said. And we don't back away from the position because the real assassinator is Bush and Cheney and the whole administration for the lives they have destroyed here and in Iraq. They're the ones. And what they refused to air which was far more provocative in my mind and in the minds of my band mates is this: this system has become so brutal and vicious and cruel that it needs to start wars and profit from the destruction around the world in order to survive as a world power. *That* is what we said. And we refuse not to stand up; we refuse to back down from that position."

There were few bands in a position of popularity who dared speak the words Rage did. When one considers the fact ex-Pantera guitarist Dimebag Darrell was assassinated for little more than finishing one band and starting another, it's clear De La Rocha could be putting his life in danger speaking out against the propaganda machine.

Though there have been commendable efforts from the likes of the Dixie Chicks – who virtually ended their career with a speech daring to oppose President Bush – there were no bands who had forceful music to accompany their strong armed opinions (perhaps with the exception of System Of A Down). Few bands can make a crowd of 10,000 bounce in unison as well as providing a stark, brutal message which needs to be heard.

Yet whenever they were pushed on their legacy and their influence, Rage would deny their palpable weight within the rock community. They would not claim they were even musically influential, much less political pioneers. It meant more to them to continue saying their piece than pontificating on their relevance and influence. They just *did* it.

"There are so many voices and so many who are doing exactly what we're doing," De La Rocha told Ben Myers in a candid interview back in 1999. "But because we're at an intersection where art and commerce collide, the massive mergers that have gone on between the major record companies have developed into a new format, a vacuum in which to sell this very poppy, very commercially-orientated music – all these one hit wonder bands. Because of that, the five major record labels have predominantly ignored a number of great bands, whether that be a Brazilian activist band or Asian Dub Foundation – people who, like us, also see music as a viable weapon in terms of politicising young people who may not have yet responded to the times and conditions in which they live. It's very important that music occupies that space. I can't say that Rage is the most important band in opening people's eyes to global concerns, we just happen to be the band who have been able to create this open space within pop music and try to set in motion a new era where more dissident voices within commercial music can come and be a part of the dialogue."

Brad Wilk also spoke for the rest of his band mates when he admitted in *Drum!* that, "there's a part of me that wants to agree with you here and say, yes, we're highly influential, but I just don't feel it. I appreciate it when people say that though. It feels nice just to be even asked a question like that. I suppose we have influenced a lot of bands who are only starting to surface now – which I guess makes our music all the more viable – but our music definitely sets us apart from everyone else."

So what of the future for Rage Against The Machine? Will they simply make their statements in a live environment or will they pledge to make new music? How long can they last the second time around? Are they still relevant in today's market?

Only the ultra cynical music fan would contest that, with the success of Audioslave, the musicians in RATM have no more to give to a reactionary style of music protest. On the contrary, maybe after their experience at the heart of the industry cogs, they have even more to say and are better placed to say it ...?

Epilogue

"The future is anything you want it to be and there is no injustice that is insurmountable if you have the courage of your convictions and are willing to take a stand."
Tom Morello

The members of Rage Against The Machine are all multi-millionaires yet all live relatively modesty. There are no twenty-five bedroomed houses, no perpetual groupies snorting cocaine off band member's behinds and no clear trappings of success. The group are pretty much the same people they were in 1992, still angry about social injustice and far more aware of how and why to pervade the system.

Their biggest problem is more in line with remaining in sync as musicians and artists, and we must all hope that the death knell for so many creative geniuses – the dreaded 'creative differences' doesn't spell the end for Rage Against The Machine (again) any time soon.

"I think there's a mutual respect for each other in this band, and especially a respect for what's happened to us," De La Rocha has said. "I don't think there's a political organization that exists that wouldn't kill for the opportunities that we now possess. Just being able to use the media the way that we do, we're really excited about the potential of it. That's what ultimately keeps it going, and I'm not afraid to say that it's the only thing that keeps it going."

Before the break up of the band, Zack's words rang with irony. "I don't think that in our heart of hearts we were ever ready to destroy this gift," he told *Kerrang!* "Right now we're taking this day by day but I don't see any reason why we can't continue to do this, primarily because we've really overcome a lot of the tensions that existed within the band around the mid-Nineties. There were definitely some very serious tensions back then, but now we're talking much more, discussing things and acting more as a collective than we ever have. Because of that, I see no reason not to continue into the future."

Yet perhaps something which can easily be forgotten is the personal feelings which exist behind the scenes. Each member of Rage is very different but the two more unsung members, Brad Wilk and Tim Commerford, perhaps remain the glue that holds the band together and are often more influential and emotional than given credit for. Commerford opened up to Ben Myers admitting, "I think about what it will be like once all this is over. My job has been to deal with the relationship between four people whilst going onstage and dealing with my own personal insecurities. That's it. That's my role. Hopefully there'll be something out there for me to do after the band, because I do worry about it. I don't worry about the money, but rather feeling good about myself and doing something I want to do. It's going to be hard after this to match everything we've achieved in Rage. I mean, playing in Rage is a skill and a craft. The prospect of what we can achieve is exciting and when that goes away we'll be over."

Rage go as far as they can within the confines of a successful rock group and, given their immense and continuing success, that is something to admire. They have no need to continue for the money, unless it is to fund their causes; they continue to upset the establishment at every available opportunity. For this alone they should be championed and held dear. Yet it's when their words and actions truly inspire action that Rage can say they have done what they set out to do and there is no doubt the tides are changing. Today, there is more unrest than ever before at the actions of the world governments and the oppression of people, of all minorities and of all colours. As we gear up for ever more massive social change and public awareness, it is only fitting that accompanying this uprising and the destruction of the system – the machine which has held us captive for too long – should be the most incendiary soundtrack imaginable. A glorious potent mixture of poetic social awareness and a thumping call for reform. As the flags burn and the mainstream media becomes obsolete, we should remember one thing and one thing only: *fuck you, I won't do what you tell me* ...

Recommended Reading

As Zack De La Rocha says, "anger is a gift". Anger and fury at the injustices of the world around us can have two potential effects, it either makes you bitter and twisted inside whereby you may feel powerless to do anything about a situation or a world out of your reach and control – or it can drive you to do something about it. Before you can do anything about anything, you need to be armed with two things – education and a willingness to change yourself. Too many people focus so hard on the particular causes that seem unjust and affect other people's lives without attempting to change their own make-up and looking within before looking outside. Change can only happen outside of your environment when you are willing to change your own. No one is perfect but we can all do something to better our lives and those of people around us. Before we can expect the world to change, we may have to alter our entire outlook.

I hope with this book you have learned a lot more about the exact beliefs and campaigning the band has taken on, and a lot more about the people they stand behind – be they Death Row prisoners or indigenous people of stolen lands …

Unfortunately I cannot go into the full extent of these situations in this book, but here are some highly recommended resources on such subjects:

BOOKS

All Things Censored, Mumia Abu-Jamal (Seven Stories Press) 2001
American Heretics: Rebel Voices In Music, Ben Myers (Codex) 2002
Bloodlines Of The Illuminati, Fritz Springmeier (Available For Free Online: www.Thewatcherfiles.Com/Bloodlines/Index.Htm)
Guerrilla Warfare, Ernesto Guevara (Souvenir Press) 2003
Health Betrayal, Eve Hillary 2007
If I Should Die: A Death Row Correspondence, Jane Officer (New Clarion) 1997
Live From Death Row, Mumia Abu-Jamal (Avon) 1996

Not On The Label: What Really Goes Into The Food On Your Plate, Felicity Lawrence (Penguin) 2004

Our Word Is Our Weapon, Jose Saramago, Subcomandante Marcos (Serpents Tail) 2002 (Zack De La Rocha has said: "Somewhere between the passionate analysis of Ricardo Flores Magón and the poetic fury of Eduardo Galeano, lie these most powerful and essential communiques of the new Mexican Revolution. Possibly the most influential collection of writings upon my musical and political perspective.")

Prison Writings: My Life Is My Sundance, Leonard Peltier (St. Martins Press) 2000

Steal This Book, Abbie Hoffman (Avalon) 2005

The Natural Way To Heal, Walter Last (Hampton Roads Publishing) 2004

Understanding Power: The Indispensable Chomsky, Noam Chomsky (Vintage) 2003

Unseen Hand: Introduction To The Conspiratorial View Of History, A. Ralph Epperson (Publius) 1985

You Are Being Lied To: The Disinformation Guide to Media Distortion, Historical Whitewashes and Cultural Myths, Russ Kick (Disinformation) 2002

VIEWING

A Place Called Chiapas (1998)
Cradle Will Rock (1999)
Fahrenheit 9/11 (2004)
Network (1976)
Paradise Lost 2: Revelations (2000)
Paradise Lost: The Child Murders At Robin Hood Hills (1996)
The Rosa Parks Story (2002)
V For Vendetta (2005)
Viva Zapata! (1952)
Zeitgeist: The Movie (2007)

MAGAZINES

Alternative Press, Billboard, DRUM!, Entertainment Weekly, Guitar One, Guitar World, Kerrang!, Metal Hammer, Nexus, Pitchfork Media, Propaganda, Raw, Raygun, Rolling Stone, Spin, Teen People.

NEWSPAPERS:

Enlace Civil, Guardian, In Jersey Rocks, New York Post, Nuevo Amanecer Press, Pravda, Times Pop.

WEBSITES

http://www.theroc.org/roc-mag/textarch/roc-03/roc03-07.htm
www.hartfordadvocate.com
www.janeganahl.com
www.theroc.org
www.youtube.com
www.web.csustan.edu/english/**reuben**/home.htm
www.mexconnect.com/mex_/travel/acogan/acbio.html